Going Through Trials with God:
7 Lessons Learned Through Shaken Baby Syndrome

Sierra Cooke

Find Sierra Online:

Instagram @sierra.m.cooke & @shaken.baby.mom

YouTube Sierra Cooke

TikTok @sierracooke

Podcast Going Through Trials with God on Spotify and Anchor

Email sierra.marie.cooke@gmail.com

Online Business / Health & Wellness Products

Book Cover photo Alyssa Jordan, Alyssa Spivey Photography

Dedication:

In loving memory of my daughter Christa, my dad Chris, my mamaw Helen, and my cousin Kerry. They all played a role in who I am today. I look forward to the day I will see them again.

FREE GIFT

I want to send you my future eBooks to your inbox for free.

https://tinyurl.com/urzmv4dc

Contents:

Hopeless, hating myself, my situation, and my life, to finding hope in Christ and learning how to love myself is how I spent most of my 20s. If you are going through a trial, this book will give you inspiration to trust and lean on God no matter what. My hope is by sharing my story, you will be able to do the same when you go through a trial. Maybe it doesn't seem like it right now, but with God, it is always possible to get off of rock bottom. I will share with you the lessons I learned through experiencing many trials, one being my daughter suffering Shaken Baby Syndrome. After reading this book, you will feel motivated to make true transformation happen in your life, through Christ. I start by sharing mine and my daughter's story with you, and then the lessons I learned along our journey. The lessons I share will benefit you whether you're going through a trial currently, or you're not yet but will one day

Section 1: Our Story

"We think you shook your daughter", are the six most traumatizing words anyone has ever said to me. After bursting out in tears and replying "I would never do that", the investigator said, "I'm sorry, I had to say that to see how you would respond. Your husband isn't responding to that like we think he should."

This is my story of how I went from being a mother of a healthy three month old child named Christa, to being a mother who had to hold that same child as she took her last breath. I'm going to share with you how shaken baby syndrome taught me many lessons. I believe these lessons will benefit you in many ways. I feel it's important to paint the full picture as I tell this story, and that will include sharing with you a little about my first marriage. After reading this, maybe you will find yourself in a similar situation, or know someone who is, and this will help you or the person you know, come to the realization that abuse is very serious, even if it doesn't seem like it in the moment, and it can have devastating consequences.

This story began when I was 19 years old. I was introduced to a man who I began dating, and although deep down I knew his behavior was manipulative, I moved into an apartment with, after only about two months of meeting him. Shortly after moving in together, I became pregnant with our first child, Brilee. A few months after that, we got married, and chose to marry each other only because I was pregnant and we thought it was the "right" thing to do. I quickly realized after we got married, that marriage didn't fix anything for us. His behavior and our relationship was still just as toxic, and the piece of paper saying we were married didn't magically change any behaviors. I look back now, and I can see how emotionally and physically abusive my now ex-husband was, but in the moment, I didn't see it. Have you ever been in a situation where you could not see the red flags until afterwards? All I saw in those moments was a man who I thought I loved, and a man who was the father of my child. I was in denial. After a few years of going through emotional and physical abuse, I decided I had no choice but to end our relationship. When I made that decision, he offered to check himself into a rehabilitation center if I would stay with him and support him. He convinced me his behavior had always been caused by drugs, and he would be a completely different person once he was "clean". So I stayed. While he was in rehab, I found out I was pregnant with our second child, Christa. When I found out I was pregnant, I was heartbroken. I was staying at my grandmother's home, and at the time I was sick, vomiting, and had to ask my aunt to get me a pregnancy test. I felt humiliated asking her to do that because I was too sick and didn't have the money to get one myself. I sobbed when I thought about the situation I was going to bring another child into. My ex-husband finished rehab, and at first it seemed he had truly changed. Our daughter Christa was born, and I hoped we were going to be able to be a loving family. I was still living in denial.

My ex-husband began drinking not long after leaving rehab, and the mental and sometimes physical abuse continued. I made the decision to separate and move in with my grandmother. This part of the story is where I share with you about one of the worst days of my life.

On May 25th, 2017, when Christa was three months old, she stayed overnight with my ex-husband, her biological father. Since we were separated at the time, he stayed in the home we owned together, and I stayed at my grandmother's. That night, I sent him a text that asked "how is Christa?" To which he responded, "she's whiny as hell". In that moment, I thought nothing of that text. I didn't realize what a red flag it was until investigators later pointed it out to me. I worked as a licensed massage therapist, and was at work doing a massage the morning of May 26th, 2017. It was a normal day until I heard a knock on the door during the massage. The director of the spa opened the door and said "your mom called, you need to get to the hospital because your baby is there". The last time I had spoken to my ex-husband was the night before. As far as I knew in that moment, he was supposed to drop Christa off at my sister's house, who was going to babysit her until I got off work. My sister had sent me a photo through text saying, "does Christa always sleep with one eyelid cracked open?" I looked at the photo and replied "no, but sometimes babies can do that". I walked out of work to my car feeling confused, and saw I had missed calls from my mom. My adrenaline began pumping when I heard the tone of her voice when she answered my call. All I can remember is hearing her yelling "get to the hospital, Christa is barely breathing, the ambulance took her there!" My mom had gone over to my sister's house to take her and Christa to get breakfast. It felt like I was a million miles away from that hospital. Once I arrived at the ER, I told the person at the desk that my daughter was there. She opened the doors, and I remember hearing a moaning sound, and I thought to myself "there's no way that's her, I've never heard a baby sound like that, it can't be her". I turned the corner, and she was lying on a hospital bed with several doctors and nurses surrounding her, and I realized the sound I heard was coming from her. A doctor approached me and asked "has she been exposed to any drugs? We think she's had a stroke; her temperature is in the low 90s, we need to do a CT scan and intubate her to try to get her stabilized." I stood and watched in shock, but I still did not realize how serious the situation was. Thoughts were racing through my mind like "this is not real, I just held my baby yesterday, she was smiling, what happened, I just want my baby to be okay". My mom and pastor, two people who at that time brought me the most comfort, arrived at the ER so I was not alone. I was asked questions by the doctors that I had no answers to, because I hadn't seen Christa in about 24 hours. My ex-husband was not present to answer any questions.

Doctors were able to intubate her and stabilize her enough for her to be transferred by ambulance to a Children's Hospital. My mom and I were not allowed to ride with her in the Lifeline Children's Hospital ambulance, so we got into my mom's car and began driving to the hospital they were taking her to. While we were in the car, I received a phone call. A nurse from the hospital emergency room that we had just left said "I need you to come back to the ER". I responded "what? Why?" she said "I can't tell you that over the phone, I just need you to come back here". I hung up the phone and told my mom to turn around and go back. When my mom asked "why?" I busted out in tears and said "the nurse said she can't tell me over the phone, I think she's dead!" When we pulled up to the ER, we were met by hospital security and a nurse. Deep down, I knew what was happening. They walked us to the consulting room. I remember thinking "no, please not this room, I know what happens in this room".

I was familiar with that room because ten years before, at age 13, I was in a room just like it when doctors told my mom and I that my dad had no brain activity after an ATV accident, and asked us if we would like to donate his organs. Once we were in the room, the nurse said "as soon as they got Christa onto the ambulance, she coded, they have been doing CPR for about 20 minutes and she still has no pulse. We wanted you to be able to say goodbye." I felt paralyzed. The image of her that flashed through my mind was horrific. I responded, "I don't want to see her like that". She said, "are you sure?" I heard in my head, what I now believe was God, say "go". My mom and I were then led to the room where the staff were doing CPR on my daughter. I believe God respected my wishes to not see her like that because all I can remember seeing was a nurse over her doing compressions, and her tiny blue hand bouncing up and down. I ran over to her, dropped to my knees, and began praying out loud. I begged God to save my baby. Praying out loud was something I had never done before that moment. I felt such deep anguish, that praying out loud and begging for her life was all I could do. After a few moments, I heard the doctor say "I have a pulse".

In those moments, I had no idea what was to come, I just knew she was alive and that was enough for me to feel some sort of relief.

Once again, the nurses put Christa onto the ambulance and took her to the closest Children's Hospital. You may be wondering where my ex-husband was through all of this. At the time, he claimed to not have a cell phone that worked without wi-fi, so communicating to him what was going on was difficult. He was at work at the time, so we were trying to communicate through the office at his place of work. When my mother and I arrived at the Children's Hospital, my ex-husband arrived there as well. We were met by a forensic medical doctor. The doctor asked us several questions which included "do you sleep with your child in the bed with you?" to which I answered "yes, I do, is that what caused this?" my stomach turned thinking I could've been the cause just by sleeping with her. She responded "it could, but we don't know enough just yet". She also asked questions about my relationship with my husband and about my older daughter, who at the time was two years old. I still had no idea what was really going on. We were finally taken back to see Christa after being questioned. I remember how it felt walking into the PICU, the pediatric intensive care unit. Just walking through there scared me because I knew being there meant something serious was going on. When we entered her room, I thought about how she looked nothing like the baby I had seen the day before. She was no longer the smiling, happy baby full of life. She had a NJ tube, aka feeding tube in her nose, her eyes were very swollen and barely open, she had a central line placed on the left side of her chest/shoulder area, she had bruises on her where nurses had tried to place an IV, she had a tube placed in her throat to breathe for her, she had restraints around her wrists holding them down, a rectal thermometer placed to constantly track her temperature, a catheter to track her urine output, an O2 sensor on her foot, and something constantly tracking her blood pressure. Christa was placed in a medically induced coma to allow her brain and body to try to begin healing. Christa's PICU doctor was in the room as we entered. I asked him "what's wrong with her?" He responded, "she has shaken baby syndrome". I turned to my ex-husband and said "did you shake her?!" He replied "no!" I had so many questions, but I can't remember if I asked any of them immediately after hearing that. I felt like I was in shock. It felt like my knees were about to buckle. I wanted to just wake up from what felt like a horrible nightmare.

Shortly after being told Christa had experienced shaken baby syndrome, we were investigated by a DCS (the department of Children's Services) caseworker and an investigator from a local police station. It was hard for me to process the fact that I was being interrogated. I just wanted to be with my baby, but instead I was in a room being questioned. They asked me where I was the night before, if I knew what happened to Christa, questions about my ex-husband, if Christa ever cried so much that it made me feel frustrated, if I ever felt depressed, and so on. At the end of questioning me, the investigator said "we think you shook your daughter". I burst out in tears and said, "I would never do that". I could tell the DCS investigator felt uncomfortable and she handed me a tissue. The investigator responded by saying "I'm sorry, I had to say that to see how you would respond. Your husband isn't responding to that like we think he should". He continued by asking me questions like "why do you think that is?" and "does your husband do drugs"? I felt so traumatized. My daughter was lying in a PICU room in a medically induced coma on life support, and I had to endure being interrogated about what happened to her. After being investigated, I tried going back to see Christa. The PICU was a locked unit, so anyone entering had to push a button and let them know who they were there to see. I pushed the button and when asked "can I help you?" I responded "I'm here to see Christa Hunt". The person on the other end replied "you can't come back yet". Many different thoughts ran through my mind including my daughter being taken away from me. Being defensive after feeling like I was being blamed for shaking Christa, I responded, "yes I can, let me in". The lady, giving no reason for why they weren't allowing me to see Christa responded, "We will let you know when you can come back", to which I responded "I have a right to be with my daughter, let me in". She hung up, and I pushed the button again, with no response. I began feeling scared that they were either taking her from me or doing something to her without my permission. I even felt like maybe she had died while I was being questioned and they weren't telling me yet. Out of desperation, I began banging on the door. Her nurse poked her head out and said "you can't do this, I am calling security", and she shut the door. In that moment, I didn't care what they were saying. I banged on the door again. This time someone else came to the door and said "the Neurologist is examining her, we will come get you as soon as he's done". I asked "why didn't someone just tell me that?! I had no idea what was going on". Security arrived, and walked me back to her room. As soon as I saw her nurse I said, "get me a copy of my rights". She did, and the first right listed said parents have a right to be with their child at all times. I circled it and told her it was my right to be in the room. I think back now to how I reacted, and if I was in the same scenario now, I feel I would react differently. I did feel bad afterward for the other patients who had to hear me banging on the door. However, I was going through a very traumatic situation and it felt to me the situation was not handled properly. That was the first of many times I had to stand up for my rights or for Christa's rights. It was the first time in my life that I truly spoke up and I was way out of my comfort zone. After apologizing, the Neurologist explained what he found during his examination. He told us Christa had severe brain damage. He explained she had a subdural hematoma, caused by her brain bouncing back and forth against her skull. He also mentioned he wasn't sure what her vision would be like, if she still had any, because there was too much blood to see if her retinas were still attached. He wasn't expecting Christa to live. He said "if she does live, she will be severely disabled and need around the clock care." Again, I was thinking about how just the day before Christa could see me, she could smile at me, she was healthy, she had her whole life ahead of her, and it was all taken away in less than 24 hours.

After the doctors' examinations and investigations were done, it was just me and her left in the room. I felt broken, confused, alone in my situation, scared, and lost. I thought to myself, "what now?" I was in a place of unknown outcomes. Sitting, waiting, crying, and praying was pretty much all I could do. My family stayed the first few nights in the waiting room. It was comforting, but they too were in the same situation. They were also experiencing the same confusion and heart brokenness I was. Christa lived through that first night, and one night quickly turned into two weeks. Staying by her side 24/7 had me feeling like my world outside of that PICU room had stopped. I couldn't go back to work, I couldn't go home to sleep in my own bed, and I couldn't be with my other daughter Brilee. I couldn't stand the thought of leaving my little 3 month old baby there alone.

You may again be wondering where my ex-husband was throughout this time. Throughout the first two weeks after Christa's injury, my ex-husband and I were still under investigation, but no custody decision had been made by DCS. He stopped by the hospital from time to time, and our daughter Brilee stayed with him a few nights at the nearby Ronald McDonald house. I think back to those moments and now I realize I was in deep denial. My brain was in survival mode, and I felt I could not accept that my husband, my daughter's biological father, shook her. I started this journey out in denial, but it did not take long for me to come out of denial and face the truth.

I began thinking back through all of my choices and things that had happened to Christa since she was born. There was a day, when Christa was about two months old, that I got home from work around 8pm and noticed the inside of Christa's ears were purple. My mother-in-law at the time watched Christa and our other child Brilee, while my ex-husband and I went to work. He called and asked her about it, and she said "oh Brilee must've done it". At that time, abuse didn't even cross my mind. I looked it up online, and when I saw that certain cancer can cause that, I got concerned. I made an appointment with her pediatrician, and when I took her, they told me she did not have insurance and they wouldn't see her without it. I was 21 years old and naive, so I took her home. I found out my ex-husband never added her to his work health insurance, so they could no longer insure her. I applied for health insurance through the state, which ended up being a blessing in disguise because it eventually helped her a lot after her injury. It took a while to get health insurance, and by then her ears were no longer purple. It lasted a few days and then went away. There was another time, after my ex-husband and I were separated and living in different houses, that I picked Christa and Brilee up from my mother-in law. Christa began projectile vomiting that night. It was so bad that I took her to a Children's Hospital emergency room. They admitted her to watch her overnight. They changed her formula, and since she seemed to be tolerating it, they discharged her to go home. My ex-husband didn't come to visit her or sit with us at any time. I now see that as a possible red flag, after what the forensic doctor told me about those two situations. The projectile vomiting happened only one week before the main event occurred when she coded and everything. After Christa experienced shaken baby syndrome and was admitted to the PICU, we told the forensic doctor about those things happening. She didn't say much other than "this could mean she was abused more than once". When I asked her "how can you know that?" She responded, "there's no way for me to be able to tell if the blood shown on the scans she had is old or new, so I don't know for sure".

One day, I was sitting in the PICU with Christa, when the forensic doctor came into the room and let me know she wanted to speak with me. I was not expecting her to say what she did. She said "do you understand that if you had gotten Christa help when she had the purple ears and when she was vomiting, she wouldn't be in this situation"? I wish I would've taken up for myself, but I was so caught off guard that I just started crying. Her saying that to me did trigger something in me to look for more answers. I went down to the records department in the hospital and requested to see her records from the night I had her in there for projectile vomiting. When I read through them, I discovered a doctor had written "swollen fontanel, may need CT". When I saw that, I thought to myself "did they miss something? They never did a CT, they just changed her formula and sent us home". I couldn't believe the forensic doctor was saying I could've gotten her help and prevented everything, when I was the one who took her to the ER for projectile vomiting. I trusted them when they sent us home saying it was just the formula. They are the experts, why didn't they see the signs if it was abuse? When I brought it to the attention of the forensic doctor after reading that, she said "there's no way for us to know".

I included this part of the story specifically because I want people to know the warning signs. I will never know for sure if the purple ears and projectile vomiting was due to abuse. I never expected my ex-husband and possibly my ex-mother-in-law to abuse Christa. I look back now and see more red flags than I did in those moments. I share the details like this part of our story because even hospital staff failed Christa. She had a swollen soft spot, they said she may need a CT scan to check it, and they didn't follow through. They never questioned why Christa's father didn't come to the hospital. His two month old was in the hospital, and he didn't come to be with her, why wasn't that a red flag to them? I want people to understand that abuse isn't always extremely obvious, and even professionals can miss it. If you or someone you know ever has a gut feeling that something is wrong, don't allow denial to keep you from taking action. It is always better safe than sorry. Start with researching and knowing the signs of abuse in children. Don't wait to do it, you never know when knowing that information can be used to help save a child's life.

Now I am going to get back to telling the story. One day, the DCS caseworker asked if my ex-husband and I would take polygraph tests. I told her I would, and I talked my ex-husband into doing one as well. On the day I was scheduled to take mine, I walked into the justice center, into a room where they asked me questions. I was asked all the questions and had to give my answer. Then, he took me into the room where the actual polygraph test took place. There was something placed around my head, something I had to sit on, place my feet on, and I had a blood pressure cuff constantly taking measurements. I felt like a criminal even though I had done nothing wrong. I had never felt so nervous in my life, and could hardly believe that I was in that position. The investigator asked the same questions as he did 30 minutes prior, before the actual test began. Then he led me back into the first room where he asked me questions, and told me to sit and wait for him to come back. He entered the room again after about 20 minutes, along with another investigator. They both told me I had passed the test only failing one question. That question was "have you ever hurt anyone?" My answer was no, but during the test I couldn't stop thinking about 7 years before when my sister and I got into a fight. He told me that all other questions revealed to them I was telling the truth, and they did not believe I had hurt my daughter. Some of those other questions included; do you know what happened to Christa on May 25th, 2017? Have you ever hurt Christa? Have you ever thought about hurting either of your children? And there were several more that I cannot remember. The entire polygraph process for me, took about two or three hours to complete. This was not the case for my ex-husband. The process took about five or six hours to complete when he went for his polygraph test. That was the first time I came out of denial enough to realize something wasn't right. When my ex-husband arrived at the Ronald McDonald house after his polygraph test, I met him with several questions. We sat in my car as I asked him "why did your test take so much longer than mine?" He responded "because they kept asking me questions". I said, "so, they asked me questions too, that doesn't explain anything, what questions did they ask?" He replied, "well they said I failed the polygraph test so they wouldn't let me leave until I told the truth." I could feel my heart start to race, "the truth? What truth?!" I said. He responded "I had Christa bouncing on my knee holding her with one hand, and I was scrolling on Facebook with my other hand. Then she all of a sudden jerked and fell on her head onto the floor". Infuriated, I replied "what!? And you're just now admitting to this? What if you had told them this at the beginning? She may not be in this position. If you had told me that evening, I would've taken her to the emergency room!" He replied "I know, I don't know why I didn't say anything". I will admit after hearing that, I responded by yelling and cussing him, telling him that I was so angry at him for withholding that information. I look back and realize I probably didn't handle that situation in the best way, and learned from it.

The next day when I saw the forensic doctor again, I asked her if Christa's injuries could've been caused by what my ex-husband said happened to her. The doctor said, "it could've made it worse, but no, Christa's injuries are equivalent to her falling off of a two-story building, dropping her couldn't have caused this". At that point, I still felt I didn't know who to believe. My mom and I were researching every possibility. We researched different things such as dropping an infant, an infant suffocating, vaccine injuries, strokes in infants, and shaken baby syndrome. I wanted to be 100% sure the doctors weren't missing something since my ex-husband wouldn't confess to shaking her. One day, the forensic doctor was in Christa's PICU room when my ex-husband was present. For whatever reason, he decided to show her a video he had recorded of her the evening she was injured. The night that she was alone with him. In that video, it showed Christa lying in his lap, with her eyes closed, one arm in the air that was moving up and down repeatedly, and she was making a monotone humming sound. I don't know exactly how to explain the sound, but she was making that sound throughout the entire five-minute video. I also heard my ex-husband talking to her and laughing. He explained he thought she was having a bad dream. The forensic doctor said she was shocked by what she saw. She showed the video to the Neurologist and he explained he believed it was a seizure, and most likely she was seizing all night, until it eventually led to a stroke. After hearing that, the image of my baby lying there, seizing, freezing cold with a temp of 94 degrees Fahrenheit, and probably all alone wondering why no one was coming to hold her, until it got so bad that she had a stroke, entered my mind. Those thoughts were almost unbearable. To this day they still bring tears to my eyes, and it's one reason I am writing this book. I pray by sharing this experience, other babies won't have to lie there like she did after being abused.

After seeing the video, the forensic doctor told the DCS investigator about it and we were questioned again. When they questioned my ex-husband, they asked to see the video. He told them he had lost the phone. When they questioned me about it, I gave them my phone, and they uploaded everything from my phone to their computer, which included my and my ex-husband's Facebook messenger conversations. After they reviewed our conversations, they questioned me about a part where on the night she was injured, May 25th, 2017, when she was alone with him, I asked him "how is Christa doing?" and he responded, "she's whiny as hell". The investigator asked me "why wasn't that a red flag to you?" I said, "I just didn't think anything of it". Of course, now when I look back, I can see it was a red flag, but in the moment I didn't. I want to point that out in case someone who is reading this is in an abusive relationship. Whenever it becomes normal to us for someone to talk in that way, it is no longer a red flag. If that was the first time he had ever spoken like that, it would've been a red flag. But for me, it wasn't because I had allowed him to speak like that to me and about me and our kids many times before. My hope is for someone out there in an abusive relationship to learn from my mistakes and realize it's not always easy to spot a red flag in the moment. I don't believe everyone who cusses when talking about their child is guilty of something, but I do believe if I had asked more questions after my ex-husband's response, I possibly could have figured out something was wrong, and intervened.

After collecting all of their information from their interviews with us and the doctors, DCS decided they believed my ex-husband shook Christa, so they filed a motion to temporarily take custody from my ex-husband, and give me full custody. The document stated my ex-husband could do supervised visits with no overnight visits. The only way to change the order that was signed by a judge, was to appear in court on the day they gave him, which was scheduled for about two weeks after receiving the order. I remember seeing my ex-husband expressing he was angry about it, and didn't want to get charged with anything and go to jail. From my observation, he planned to show up to court and fight against the order. I believe it was around the time they served him those papers that I began coming further out of denial and opening my eyes to some things that I considered to be red flags. When I started to notice my ex-husband's behavior, the words of the investigator came to mind "your husband isn't acting like we think he should". I thought maybe the investigator was right. I noticed my ex-husband was doing things that could compromise his ability to see our children. I could hardly believe he was coming into her PICU room smelling like weed, knowing the investigators told him he would have to do random drug tests. We argued about it several times. I also started noticing how his family was acting. His mother came to see Christa a few times along with my ex-husband, and she never shed a tear. My ex-husband would be standing over her bed crying, and she would say things like "hurry up, I gotta get back home". I thought to myself, "what kind of mother shows no emotion for her son nor her own granddaughter in this situation"? The question the investigator asked kept playing in my mind. After some time, I started believing my ex-husband and some people in his family were not acting how I think they should've been in that situation.

After about a total of a month in the hospital, Christa was able to go home with me. During her hospital stay, she had gone from being fully supported by a vent, to coming off of that vent, to having a feeding tube placed in her stomach, to opening her eyes, to going through a lot of storming, (the brain firing random signals causing the body to tense up), to being discharged. She was discharged with the diagnosis of subdural hematoma, seizures, feeding tube dependency, blindness, and global cortical ischemia. Once Christa was discharged, I was her full-time caregiver. We went back to my grandmother's house after discharge, and at that time I had no idea Christa was eligible for nursing care. No one at the children's hospital had mentioned that to me. No one discharging her had set that up for her. So, we went home with me truly not knowing fully how to care for her, as she required around the clock care. I later found out Christa had gastroparesis, but at the time of discharge she was not diagnosed with it, and that caused us many issues. At first, everything that was going through her G-tube was coming back up. We were feeding her directly into her stomach since she had a G-tube. I later found out that all along, she should have been fed directly into her intestines, through what doctors call a G-J tube. She was constantly experiencing pain because of reflux and vomiting. She was also still storming and still having seizures. Christa was taking about 10 medications, and at that time, I was not able to go back to my massage therapy job because I had to take care of her full time. I did not mind doing that, but I knew that that was not sustainable long-term. I knew that if Christa were to live for years, there would be no way for me to sustain being a caregiver 24/7 and not working. That made me feel very hopeless. I felt exhausted. I felt confused as to how that could be my life, and how I was ever going to get out of that situation. I ended up taking Christa to a hospital about two hours away from where we lived to attempt to get a second opinion. She saw a Neurologist there, and she said after reviewing her documents, she also believed Christa's injuries were from shaken baby syndrome.

I survived those first few months financially by receiving government assistance. At the time, I was a very angry person. I was in a position where I felt I was paying the consequences for someone else's choice. I harbored a lot of anger during that season of life. The court order, that had been signed by a judge before we ever even went to court, stated that my ex-husband was not allowed to visit with our children overnight, and that it would be supervised visitation at my discretion because the children were put into my custody until it could go through court. Shortly after Christa was released from the hospital, I went to do a supervised visitation with her biological father. At that visit he decided to tell me, "I actually didn't even drop Christa, they wouldn't let me leave so I had to make up a lie. I was livid. I told him "You're never going to see these kids again". Little did I know then, a few years later that would become his reality through a step-parent adoption.

A few months after Christa was discharged, after my ex-husband had postponed it, we finally went to court over the situation. My ex-husband did retain an attorney. That time in court was supposed to determine what the ongoing custody arrangements would be, and also to decide if criminal charges needed to be issued. I was extremely nervous walking into that courtroom. I was so afraid that somehow, they would give him some type of custody. I was also hopeful that he would get jail time for what he did. At that time, I had been her caregiver for months, and I realized the depth of what had truly happened. I wanted him to suffer the consequences of his actions. I wanted him to be punished for what he was forcing me and Brilee to go through daily with Christa's condition. I testified against him, and had every intention of doing whatever I could to get justice served. I was there, but it was DCS taking him to court. It wasn't me taking him to court so I really did not have a say in whatever happened. We sat in there for I think about six hours. It felt like it drug on forever. I do remember one thing he said specifically when asked why he allowed Christa to lie there seizing all night. The DCS attorney was questioning my ex-husband about the night he was alone with Christa. He admitted that he knew something was wrong, because she wouldn't wake up or eat at one point, so he splashed water on her face. The DCS attorney said "if you knew something was wrong, why didn't you call your wife"? My ex-husband responded "because I didn't want to hear her gripe at me". It was hard for me to believe how selfish he was. It's difficult for me to remember everything that was said during that time. They made everyone leave the room except for me and him. I had no one there to try to help me to remember what was said. There was so much said that I thought for sure my ex-husband was going to be convicted of something. I thought he basically convicted himself because he just kept talking and talking.

At the end of the day, the DCS worker who I had known through all the investigations, and the attorneys and the judge all went to a room to make a decision. I had to sit out in the hallway with my ex-husband. I had every expectation that they were going to cut off his rights. I assumed they were going to take all rights, custody, and that he was going to be serving jail time. The DCS worker came out and told me they made a deal. His attorney, their attorneys, they all made a deal. She told me the judge said that we could take this case to trial, but if DCS did not win, and he won, it would be like nothing happened. It'd be a regular divorce custody agreement such as every other weekend.So DCS decided to offer a deal to my ex-husband's attorney. The deal was to keep the court order the way it was with supervised visits at my discretion, and they would not try to press criminal charges. He and his attorney accepted that. I felt devastated. I told the DCS worker it wasn't fair, and her response was "there are children who their own parents commit sex crimes against them, and their parents get custody back of them." I was horrified and stood there in shock. A sense of hopelessness washed over me. I thought to myself "I am going to have to deal with my ex-husband for possibly the next 16 years, until my kids become adults, I can't do this".

I felt so betrayed. I felt angry and I was mad at God. The court orders also allowed my ex-husband to potentially be able to petition the court. They stated, if he completed drug and alcohol classes, anger management classes, received counseling and followed all recommendations, he could petition the court to ask to gain custody back. That terrified me. The thought of Christa and Brilee being alone with him again made me want to throw up. I felt so sick thinking about how vulnerable especially Christa was, and how she probably wouldn't survive an unsupervised visit with him. It felt so unfair. My daughter had a stroke in his care, and he was only charged with neglect, and a chance to possibly get custody back of our children. I left that day so angry. Angry at the court system, at God, at myself, and at my ex-husband

Once our preliminary hearing at court was over, my ex-husband began harassing me through text message and Facebook about how he won in court. He would say things like "we won, now just wait until I take you back to court to get custody of my kids, I'm taking the classes". He would attempt to threaten me into what he wanted me to do by saying he was going to take me back to court if I didn't do it. I did respond a few times to his texts saying things like "how can you call that a win? You don't have any custody of your children." Responding to his harassing messages never helped anything. I eventually decided to only have contact with them when it was strictly about when and where we would meet for supervised visitations. We usually met once a month at a public location like a park or restaurant. He brought Brilee a toy every time we met. It bothered me because instead of truly trying to get to know Brilee and develop a meaningful relationship, he would try to basically buy her love. When Brilee was two and three years old, she didn't mind going to the supervised visits. Around the age of four, she seemed to be uncomfortable meeting with him. She would say things like "can you or Canyon play with me too?" and "I just don't feel like going".

Throughout those few years, I was in constant prayer asking God to protect us during meetings. I also begged Him to protect us from my ex-husband filing a petition to get custody back. I asked God to make a way for us to get out of that situation completely. I felt afraid each time we had to go to a supervised visit. I thought to myself "what if he's high in cocaine or meth this time, and he takes off with Brilee?" I had to pray asking God to help me let go of the "what ifs".

The first several months after Christa was discharged from her month hospital stay, we were living with my grandmother. At first, my ex-husband had moved in with his mom, so the girls and I moved back into the house he and I bought together. One day, after he followed me home, rolled the window down in his car, and yelled things at me like "you're going down", I decided I couldn't stay there. We then moved in with my grandmother. I still felt like I was in such a desperate situation because my grandmother was terminally ill, and we were staying in a very small bedroom. I knew we couldn't stay there long, but I couldn't even work, so I felt hopeless. During that time, I happened to come across a treatment for brain injuries called Hyperbaric Oxygen Therapy. A Neurologist in New Orleans was doing the treatments. It was the only place I could find to do it for Christa. I knew I had to do whatever possible to get her those treatments. With the help of my mom and some friends, we did a fundraiser in my hometown of Tellico Plains, TN, and we raised about $6,000 of the $10,000 needed. It was during that time that I also came even more out of denial about my ex-husband. He knew I needed $10,000 for Christa's treatments. That was just to cover the doctor expenses and oxygen therapy. I knew I needed more for gas, food, bills, etc. as the treatments were going to be for two months. I had asked my ex-husband to sell his second vehicle, which would've given us about $15,000. When I asked, he said "wait until you do your fundraiser to see how much you get". He posted his vehicle for sale on Facebook and said he was selling it to get his daughter treatments. I saw dozens of comments about buying it on that post. He never said anything else about it, and when I asked him about it, he said "I sold it". He refused to tell me who he sold it to.

He also said he wasn't going to give me any of the money. That he would write a money order directly to the doctor. When he asked me how much I had received at the fundraiser, I told him about $5,000. I felt if I didn't lie to him, he would've withheld that money, and I would've struggled to make it to Louisiana. So he did end up writing a money order for a few thousand dollars directly to the doctor. I found out afterwards that my ex-husband's mom had gotten a loan to buy his vehicle, and gave the vehicle right back to him, plus the money for it. In my opinion, that was her enabling him. Constantly enabling him was why he was the way he was. I know, because I had enabled him for a long time too, until I came out of denial. Overall, Christa's treatments and my expenses ended up covered, which I was so thankful for.

Not long before we were going to leave for New Orleans, Christa was admitted back into the hospital for vomiting. I believe that hospital stay was God-sent because it got us nursing care. One day while the nurse at the hospital was evaluating Christa, I asked "is it okay to submerge her feeding tube area in water to give her a bath?" She replied "doesn't her home health nurse do that?" I said "what do you mean? I didn't know she could get nursing care". She said "I can't believe they discharged you from here without setting up home health care first". She called the social work department which talked to me about nursing care. Christa qualified for it and I had no idea. I was frustrated with the hospital because I knew they had to have known this was something she qualified for. Yet they sent us home without even mentioning it. I'll never know for sure, but at times I wondered if they withheld information like that because of the situation. Christa suffered shaken baby syndrome, and as humans, it had to be difficult to not treat me as a horrible person who "let it happen". The state insurance approved Christa to have 36 hours of nursing care per week. It allowed me to end up going back to work part time, which was great, but she still required around the clock care outside of those 36 hours.

We ended up getting discharged from the hospital after a few days, and we went down to Louisiana. At first, Christa and I were going to stay at the Ronald McDonald house if there was a room available. It was first come first serve, so we had no way of knowing for sure if we'd have a room. We couldn't afford a hotel room for two months. God worked out a miracle because the clinic called me asking if I'd be interested in staying with a man whose daughter had the same treatments several years prior. He wanted to volunteer to host a family coming for treatments. I thought to myself "I really don't have a choice, so I'm just going to trust God and stay with him. The man's name was Tim. We got to his home in NOLA, and I quickly realized how big of a blessing God gave Christa and I. Tim and his family welcomed us with open arms, and loved on Christa during our stay. We started the hyperbaric oxygen therapy treatments, which were Monday-Friday for one hour a day. It was a tough thing to go through as a mom, because

Christa would sometimes cry the entire time we were in the oxygen chamber.

One night Christa was throwing up what I thought looked like blood. I took her to the ER, and they said to follow up with a GI doctor. That was hard to do since we weren't going back home any time soon. I decided to take Christa to see a GI doctor, and several specialists while we were there, to get second opinions about the vomiting, her medications, and therapies. The GI doctor asked me "how many times do you vent her stomach throughout the day?" I was confused and told her "None, because I never knew I was supposed to do that". She replied "she has no way of getting her gasses out of her stomach, so you need to vent it by opening her g-tube port several times a day". Just learning that was worth going to see the doctor because it made a huge difference in how much Christa was crying. I also had to deal with some guilt, knowing up until that point, she had been in pain from the gas that I wasn't letting out. She didn't vomit anymore after I began venting her. She also saw an orthopedic doctor, who diagnosed her with Cerebral Palsy. I was thankful we took the time to take her for the second opinions.

While I was in Louisiana, I was also going back and forth with my attorney, who was in Tennessee, trying to move forward with my divorce. She told me she expected our divorce to be final within a few months. I felt like my ex-husband still held that over me, and I was more than ready to break those chains he had on me. I wanted to move on with my life, so I decided I was going to ease my way into a friendship with someone, in hopes that in the future it would turn into more. I started a Christian Mingle account, and that was how I met my now husband, Canyon. We began by just talking about random things about the Bible and getting to know each other. I deleted my dating account and decided I would let God decide if He wanted Canyon to continue being part of my life. I gave Canyon my phone number and we talked from time to time. He agreed to set boundaries and be friends only until my divorce was final. It really helped distract me while I was in Louisiana. I had great people around me, but it still felt lonely because of the situation I was in. He was the only man who messaged me on Christian Mingle, that never talked about my physical appearance. That stood out to me. It made me respect him more. After getting to know Canyon and his heart, I just knew he would be my husband one day, even though there were no real signs of it happening.

We completed the oxygen therapy treatments, and headed back to Tennessee. I started working again as a Licensed Massage Therapist, and we established nursing care for Christa. Christa ended up back in the hospital for a virus, and while there, I asked the social worker if I could somehow get Christa more nursing hours. She introduced me to an attorney named Alex Brinson, who advocated for patients like Christa. He ended up getting us more nursing hours by filing an appeal against the state's decision to only give Christa 36 hours per week. It was then that I realized I wasn't just a caregiver for Christa, I was also an advocate for her wellbeing. Being an advocate was out of my comfort zone, but I realized I had to start speaking up for her. After Christa was discharged from the hospital, I began searching for an apartment for us to move into. Living with my grandmother was no longer sustainable for her health. I was able to find an apartment, so we moved in and it took a while to get settled. I can admit it was difficult being a single mom with two kids relying on her. I had to swallow my pride and apply for food stamps to help us survive.

A year after Christa was hospitalized after being shaken, she began vomiting. It was a red flag because it was rare for her to vomit. It was a Friday night, so I called the on-call GI doctor, who said it was normal for someone with her condition, and I could make an appointment for them to see her on Monday. I went to work the next morning, and the vomiting continued throughout the day. When I got home that evening, I called the GI doctor again. I explained that she was acting lethargic, was vomiting bright yellow liquid, and she had a vein on her chest that was bulging. He assured me she was fine, and that the yellow liquid was just stomach bile, which is normal for someone who doesn't take anything by mouth. He said I could go to the ER, but he'd recommend avoiding the ER if possible. Around midnight, I decided to take her to the ER. I had to call my mom and ask her to go with me because I was so exhausted, I felt like I couldn't even carry her. My aunt came to take Brilee to her house. When we got to the ER, they ran all of their normal tests. They said nothing seemed out of the ordinary with her blood work. I knew something was wrong though. At that point, she had brown liquid pouring out of her mouth and her g-jtube hole in her stomach. Her stomach was so swollen. I didn't know what, but I told them she was not okay. They agreed to admit her and watch her for a few days. We finally got into a room around 6am. She continued to physically look worse, but they said her bloodwork was fine. I laid down to try to take a nap, and not long after, they came rushing into the room saying she has to go for a Stat CT scan. Her blood levels that morning when they took them again were showing organ failure. I felt very confused, yet also relieved they were finally understanding that something was wrong.

She came back from the CT scan, and a PICU doctor came down to try to find a vein to put an IV in, because she was going back for emergency surgery. The doctor told me "We found out that Christa's intestines are extremely swollen, pushing on her organs, and we have to take her back for emergency surgery. We have already called the surgeon on-call and he's on his way." The anesthesiologist approached me and asked me to sign an anesthesia waiver. He circled the word death listed under possible side effects. He said "I want you to fully understand it is highly likely this will be the outcome. We are going to do our best, but there is no guarantee with her situation". I said "okay". My knees were shaking, I was sweating, and I felt I could pass out at any moment. I remember thinking and praying "please not like this Lord. Don't let her die like this". I leaned over the rail on her crib, and I told her "Christa, I love you so much. If you need to go, it's okay. You're fighting so hard baby. I love you." I had my aunt, who came to trade places with my mom, record me telling her goodbye, because I was convinced, I wouldn't see her alive again. It felt traumatizing to go from doctors saying they couldn't find anything wrong with her, to she's dying and we need to do emergency surgery. I walked with her until we got to the surgery room doors. I kissed her head and said "mommy loves you Christa".

I contacted some of the people closest to me and some of them came to sit with me in the surgery waiting room. With it being a Sunday, we were the only ones there. We prayed, and just sat silent waiting. I remember trying to fight the thoughts that were popping into my head. I kept thinking of how it was going to feel walking out of there with an empty car seat, that she should've been in. I wondered how my body would react when the surgeon came out and told me she was gone. We began praying out loud, and I remember praying "Lord, I know she's not mine, she's yours. I know you will do what's best for her. I want to keep her here, but I give this over to you. I want her to be here with me, but I also don't want her to suffer anymore. I'll trust your decision". I had the awareness that I had zero control in that situation. The only control I had was whether or not she was a DNR. At that time, she wasn't a DNR because I felt she deserved the chance to fight for her life. The surgeon, with the most fitting name, Dr. Angel, came out and let us know what happened. He explained she was still in a very bad condition, but she survived the surgery. He was able to cut out the part of her intestine that was infected. He explained that because intestines are so fragile and complex, he could not just sow them back together. He had to put them into a bag hanging outside of her body, and they would stay there until healed enough to sow back together. He said "this type of surgery on a child her age is very rare, so we don't know what to expect". My heart felt happy to hear the words "she's alive", but I was also hurt to know her body was going through so much. We walked through the hallways to the PICU, and I was praying "Lord, please help me, I'm so tired and scared". We walked into the room, and she was lying on the crib, bright lights shining down on her, a vent coming from her mouth, bruises from trying to get an IV stick, her hands and legs tied down to the bed, she was in a medically induced coma, and her intestines were sitting in a bag that was halfway inside and halfway outside her body. The bag was held up by strings that attached to the corner poles on the hospital crib. I could feel my body shaking. I was trying to be strong for Christa, yet my body wanted to collapse into a bed and sleep for days. After a few days of no changes, I started thinking back to what if I had waited like the GI doctor suggested? Christa most likely would've smothered from the inside, and died very painfully, possibly while I was sleeping. As parents, we have to listen to our intuition. If you feel like something may be wrong, don't let someone brush you off just because they are a medical professional. It's always better safe than sorry. I have received comments and messages on social media about this situation. People are quick to judge, and say things like "you're a horrible person for forcing her to go through that, why didn't you just let her die? And stuff like that. The answer to that is simple. I felt the only one who had authority over whether Christa lived or died was God. I refused to sit back and allow her to die by neglecting getting her medical treatment when needed. To me, it was already unfair that another person's choice got her into the position she was, and I wasn't going to add to that when she was fighting to live. If God wanted her to die, He would've taken her during surgery is how I see it.

After a few more surgeries and 89 days in the hospital, Christa was discharged. I felt so much freedom walking out of there, and gratitude for all the amazing people who helped us in our time of need. A few weeks after returning home, things seemed to be going well. We had an awesome nurse Deb (who ended up staying with us for years, until Christa passed away). I worked as much as I could, and Brilee went to daycare during the daytime. Life was pretty mundane for a while. I would go to work, pick

Brilee up, go home, the nurse would leave, and I would take over as Christa's caregiver. Christa's daily life involved receiving medications every 4-6 hours, receiving formula through a continuous feeding pump, being repositioned every 2-4 hours, having her nose suctioned, her mouth cleaned, and having her diaper changed often. Sometimes she also went to physical and aquatic therapy, specialist doctor visits, for a walk in her wheelchair stroller, and was given a bath in her shower chair. Every four months, Christa had to have her G-Jtube replaced under anesthesia. Seeing Christa, the way she was, lying in bed unable to move, crying a lot, blind, and fully relying on other people took a toll on my mental health. It was so hard to manage. I had to rely on God and prayer to get me through day to day. I hated living in such an unknown time. I had no idea every morning when I woke up if we'd have to go to the hospital. Sometimes I wondered if there would be a day where I woke up to Christa not breathing in her bed. God was the only way I made it through day after day, week after week, year after year.

My divorce was final a year after I had filed. It took longer than expected, and I anxiously waited for it to be finalized. Canyon and I had spoken a few times, and I was curious to see if he would act differently after my divorce was final. In my mind, I had waited long enough, and I thought God would send Canyon to me shortly after my divorce. That didn't happen as I planned. Canyon did not show interest in me other than having an occasional conversation about something Theological, because he enjoyed talking about that topic. I deeply desired a husband. I was sick of being alone, and I wanted my children to have a Godly father in their lives. I wanted them to see what a healthy marriage looked like. I also didn't want to keep doing things alone as a single mom. I kept waiting and praying for God to send Canyon to me. I had to learn how to be happy and whole as a single mom. It took a lot of inner work for me to be happy. If I scrolled through social media, I had to work on not getting jealous when I saw two people getting married. I had to learn how to have empathy for others. I would see someone on social media talking about how horrible their day was because their child had a fever, and it would frustrate me. I'd think things like "I wish my child only had a fever, you should be thankful." Those were toxic thoughts that I had to work through on a daily basis. God was teaching me how to have self-control, how to not compare situations, and how to love others. During that time, I also grew tired of waiting for God to send me a husband. I got on a dating website, went on a few dates with someone, ignored some red flags that I noticed, and grew a little attached to having someone to talk to daily. It got to a point where I could no longer ignore the red flags. The entire time I'd be with him, I'd have the thought of how that was supposed to be Canyon. I just somehow knew Canyon would be my husband one day, and no other man could measure up to him. I ended that relationship and felt hurt. I questioned God's timing. After a few weeks of feeling sorry for myself, I was alone one night at my apartment, other than

Christa being there, and I started sobbing feeling overwhelmed with my situation. I fell on my face in full surrender to the Lord. I thanked him for all He had done, and told Him I fully surrendered my dating life to Him. No matter how long I had to wait, I would wait for His perfect timing.

My grandmother passed away in 2019, and I was going to her house to get some of my stuff. On my way there, I felt like God told me to text Canyon. I did, and he called me just to catch up. We ended up talking for 2 hours, and we never stopped talking daily after that. I believe that was God's perfect timing because in the middle of experiencing such a difficult loss, He gave me the gift of Canyon. We met in person a few months later. We got engaged and then got married in September of 2019. God's timing played a huge role in our relationship because if we had waited, Canyon would not have gotten to experience being a father to Christa. Not long after we got married, we found out I was pregnant. I was extremely sick during that time. Canyon had to take care of me, Brilee, and Christa. At 11 weeks pregnant, I woke up to blood on my bed. I went to the emergency room, and they did an ultrasound. Canyon was at work at the time, so my mom went with me. I wasn't expecting the doctors to come in to tell me I was having a miscarriage, and the baby had no heartbeat. I had to call Canyon and ask him to come straight to the ER. When he came into the room and asked what's going on I told him "The baby has no heartbeat". It broke my heart when he replied "yes it does, we just heard it a few days ago". I was given medication to take at home to start contractions, to attempt to get the baby and placenta out. At that time, Christa seemed to be doing fine. I took the medication, the baby came out, and I returned to the doctor to have an ultrasound done to make sure nothing was left behind. The doctor told us I needed to have a D&C done, and that I potentially had a partial molar pregnancy, which was very rare. We got home from the doctor, and Christa suddenly had a very difficult time breathing. She was admitted and placed on a vent in the PICU for a respiratory issue. They tested her for all known viruses, and none came back positive. I went home one day to rest, and as I was at home, the doctor called and said he had to turn the vent all the way up and wasn't sure if she was going to make it through the night. I went back to the hospital to stay with her. She survived, but had to stay in the hospital for a while. I had to leave her in the PICU to go have my D&C procedure done. I was physically and emotionally exhausted. I was very upset at the fact that I was grieving the loss of my baby, having surgery done, and my other baby was lying in the PICU on a vent.

A few days after my D&C procedure, I was sitting in the PICU when the doctor called to tell me I had a partial-molar pregnancy. They suggested I go in to have my blood drawn weekly to make sure it didn't cause cancer. It seemed like things couldn't get much worse. My blood work eventually showed my HCG levels went back down to normal, so the cells from the partial-molar pregnancy didn't turn into cancer. Christa was discharged from the hospital after about a month. After that, she was not admitted to the hospital for about 6 months, which was good for her and her situation. Things seemed normal with her. We lived day to day, and still had no clue if she would live one more year, or 20 more years.

One night, after the nurse left, I walked into Christa's room to find white liquid all over her. It took my brain a minute to register that she had thrown it up. It was very unusual for her, because she never had anything in her stomach, her feeding tube bypassed her stomach. I took her to her pediatrician who said she didn't feel right about it, and thought it could be a very serious issue. I kind of thought she was exaggerating, because she had only been Christa's pediatrician for a few months. The doctor told me to take her to the emergency room. I really did not want to do that over her vomiting only one time. My husband Canyon took her to the ER, and they admitted her for observation. In the moment, I couldn't see what a miracle that hospital visit was. I had been trying for months to get Christa on palliative care, so she could be prescribed pain medication. In our state, because of the opioid crisis, pediatricians could not prescribe children pain medication. I was told Christa would have to be put on palliative care to receive pain medication. The issue was, I would have to drive two hours away to the closest palliative care pediatrician to get her put on it. Christa had a dislocated hip from all the storming that happened when she was first injured, so car rides were painful for her. Once Christa was admitted, the doctors thought there was a correlation between her vomiting and her body temperature. They believed she had vomited up fluid from her lungs and her constant low body temperature, which ranged from 88 degrees Fahrenheit to 94 degrees Fahrenheit, was part of her body beginning to shut down. Her O2 levels were also in the 80s-90s. The doctors determined they had enough evidence to place Christa on hospice care. They were going to discharge her the next day, after I went to sign the papers. I saw that as an absolute miracle. I had been trying to get her on palliative care, and just by her vomiting once and us taking her to the hospital, she got the care she needed through hospice. I am extremely grateful to God for setting all of that up in His perfect timing, because pain medication was essential when she began passing away. If God had not given us that opportunity, the last few days of her life would've been a lot different. Christa was admitted to the hospital on September 28th, 2020, mine and Canyon's one year wedding anniversary, and she was discharged with hospice care the next day. Even though she was on hospice care, we still couldn't predict how long she had left here on earth.

Having hospice care gave us access to help Christa transition pain-free through different medications that we never had access to before. She seemed to be comfortable, but I still had a difficult time leaving our house. I worried she would pass away when I was gone, or that it would happen when my husband wasn't there with us. At that point, it had been close to a year since my ex-husband had seen either of our children in person. After Canyon and I got married, he basically did not put in effort into doing supervised visits. I sent him a text to the last number he had messaged me from. I let him know what was going on, and told him he could video chat to tell her goodbye if he wanted to. I didn't hear anything back from him, so I went ahead and posted the situation to my social media accounts.

Christa seemed to be declining with each day that went by. I felt terrified of what I knew I was about to witness. I didn't know if she would be in pain or if she would be scared. I didn't know how I would react. I assumed once she took her last breath, my body would finally release the trauma it held on to for years. The night before Christa passed away, I asked Canyon to give me some alone time with Christa. Brilee was already gone on vacation with our friend Season, which was also something God worked out for us in His perfect timing. I had a friend, who lost a child herself, tell me about how she talked to her daughter and told her it was okay to go. She said to me "maybe that's what Christa is waiting for". So I went into Christa's room, I turned on some Christian worship music, and I prayed. I begged God to help Christa pass away peacefully. I even asked Him for it to be at night, when the world was asleep and everything was calm. I talked to Christa and told her how much I loved her, and that it was okay for her to let go. I told her she was so strong, and she had fought so hard. I told her I was sorry I wasn't there to protect her from shaken baby syndrome. I told her I was sorry she didn't get to live a long, healthy life. I told her she didn't deserve anything that happened to her. I told her there were so many people who cared about her. I told her how much she had saved me and changed my life forever. I told her a man named Jesus would be coming to get her soon and take her to a place called heaven. I told her she would love it because she'd meet her papaw Chris, her cousin Kerry Ray who she was named after, her baby brother Tekoa, and other family members. I told her I was so excited for her because she would be able to laugh, walk, run, and play for the first time ever. I told her I wish I could go with her, but I couldn't. I told her she can finally let go, and that I would be okay and see her again one day. I was in her room praying, talking to her, and crying for hours. I looked at and kissed her tiny feet, thinking about how soon I would never be able to do that again. I finally went to lie down in my bed, and I prayed she would not pass away while I was sleeping.

The next day, Christa had several episodes where she would tense up really hard, hold her breath and turn purple. When she caught her breath again, she would scream. I prayed "not like this Lord, please not like this". It seemed like she was trying to die, and then would catch her breath again. There was a longer duration of time between her respirations, and when she did take a breath, it was more like a gasp. The hospice nurse came to check on her, and he said he could tell there was a change. He said she had less blood circulation in her arms and legs. I asked my mom to stay the night, because I had a feeling she may not make it through the night. I still didn't know for sure if she was going to pass away. Part of me was still in denial. She had been in so many situations where she was supposed to pass away and didn't, that my mind kept saying "is she really going to die? She didn't all those times before". I was also living in fear of how deeply I was going to be hurting. I made sure to take a shower that evening, because I knew if she passed, I wouldn't be showering for days after. My mom got to our house to sit with Christa, and I tried to rest. I felt like I couldn't rest no matter how hard I tried. Canyon and I just sat silently as time passed. Christa did the thing where she was turning purple and then catching a breath a few more times. I felt in my heart she was trying to die. I talked to my friend who had been a hospice nurse, and had a son of her own pass away. I described what was going on, and she said it sounded like she was trying to transition, but the oxygen kept hitting her and making her take a deep breath. At that time, her Oxygen levels were around 60 to 70. When she would hold her breath, it would drop to the 40s. The doctors had given me the option to use or not to use Oxygen, as a comfort measure. So I decided to remove her Oxygen to see what would happen. The second I took it off, her Oxygen level began dropping and her respirations slowed even further. A part of me was screaming on the inside to put the Oxygen back on her, but I knew she was trying to go, and the Oxygen wouldn't save her, it was only prolonging what was going to happen anyway. The desperate mom in me wanted to put it back on, but the logical part of me knew it was hurting her, not helping her. We could see an immediate change in her. We then knew she was truly dying. I was beyond terrified, but I knew I had to keep it together for her. I wanted to run away or wake up from my nightmare, but she needed me, so I got into her bed and held her. That was around 7pm on October 12th, 2020. There were a few times during her time of transition that she seemed to freak out for a moment, so we immediately gave her medications to help calm her down. I held her and I sang to her. I couldn't think of anything else to sing to her except singing "we love you, you're okay" over and over while rocking her in her bed. When she would grimace, it took every ounce of strength for me to not start sobbing. After a few hours, I was getting tired. Her skin was starting to turn and stay a purple color. With each breath she took I wondered if it would be the last. I didn't know what to expect. She grimaced again, and my mom started crying. I called out to God saying "please Lord, come! Where are you? Please come now!" We called our pastor, David, to come be with us. He dropped everything and came. I had flashbacks of being by my dad's hospital bedside at the age of 13, telling him goodbye for the last time. I could hardly wrap my head around being in a similar position, with the same people, but it was then my daughter we were saying goodbye to.

Around 1am, her respirations slowed dramatically. It felt agonizing waiting to see if she was going to take another breath. It was complete silence, and then she would gasp, and then silence again. I kept praying "come on God, you showed up for me when she came into this world, I know you're going to show up as she leaves this world." I didn't hear anything for what felt like a few minutes, around 3am. I was watching, waiting for her chest to rise. All of a sudden, she made a sound, that I found out afterwards, is called the death rattle. After watching her for a few minutes, seeing she was no longer taking a breath, I knew that she was gone. She fought to live until her very last breath. Her body failing her made her death inevitable, it wasn't a lack of will to fight to live. I called out to God saying "thank you Jesus, thank you!" I held her limp hand and thought about how that was the first time since her injury that I felt her hand limp and not clinching into a fist. I felt an overwhelming joy knowing she was seeing the face of God. I imagined her running to Jesus. I also felt an overwhelming sorrow. I sobbed over her one of the first times since she was injured. I let my emotions flow out of me. We called hospice care who told us a nurse would be there in about two hours. I held her in my arms. I stared at her, because I knew it would be the last time I'd see her. I touched her hair, her arms, her hands, her legs, and her feet. I knew I never wanted to forget what she looked like and felt like. I kept thinking to myself "how will I live the rest of my life never seeing her again? I can't do this". It felt like torture. My heart was completely shattered and yet I had peace that surpassed all understanding because I knew she was finally free. It still didn't feel real. Part of me felt completely numb. I was so afraid of fully feeling my emotions. My heart was aching so badly. I didn't want her to be gone. I wanted her to be with me, as the happy, healthy three year old she was supposed to be. In those moments, I realized nothing on the planet mattered more than my relationship with Jesus. That relationship was the Only thing that got me through deep anguish.

When Christa left this earth, she took a part of me with her. A part of my heart, my being, will be with her forever. I felt like I wanted to die and go with her. The hospice nurse arrived, checked her, and called her time of death. She then asked us to collect any narcotics, and pour them out. I don't know how I was functioning at all at that point. The nurse said, "she needs to go to the forensic center for an autopsy". I assumed it was because she had been abused in the past. I replied "okay". Around 6am, an ambulance came to take her to the place where the autopsy would be done. They entered her room and my thoughtful husband said "Sierra, do you want to go on outside so you won't have the memory of them carrying her out of here?" I waited outside. They put her in a body bag, and brought her out to put her into the ambulance. When they shut the doors, I had to hold myself back from going with her. My mind kept screaming "you have to go with her!" As if she was alive. I was still trying to convince myself that she was truly gone that time, and she was never coming back. I watched the ambulance drive away. I could hardly believe my three year old was in a body bag being taken to have an autopsy done. It wasn't fair.

Canyon and I walked back into our home. It felt so empty. There were no more sounds coming from her room. No more oxygen machine running, no more noises from her, no more tv sounds from a nurse watching tv. I stood in my kitchen with my hands over my face, crying, thinking "what now?" I just stood there crying feeling paralyzed. With my eyes closed, I saw a little girl with brown hair, a white dress, and bare feet walk up to me and hug me. I couldn't see her face, but I believe it was Christa. I then felt like I could lie down and try to sleep. Before falling asleep, I sent a text to my ex-husband to let him know Christa passed away. He never responded. I woke up a few hours later, and still wondered "what now"? I stood staring at her bedroom door, wondering how I could ever manage to go in there again, with all of her stuff, but no Christa. I knew I had to go in to pick out her last outfit. Canyon went into her room with me and I broke down. All I could say was "my baby" over and over. I had made the decision to not run away from my feelings, but to let them come and let them out.

Brilee came home a few days after Christa passed away. At that time, Brilee was 5 years old. She did not know Christa passed away. The last she knew was that Christa was very sick, and the new nurses were coming to check on her because of it. Brilee had a good relationship with Christa's nurses, so I knew I had to tell her immediately, or she would've run into Christa's room to find she was not there. I asked Brilee to sit on the couch with me, and I told her that Christa went to be with Jesus, and mamaw and Tekoa in heaven. She was pitiful. She responded "can you put me to bed"? I had never heard her say that before then. I lied in my bed with her, and she started crying. I just held her. I was also very afraid of Brilee's emotions and thoughts about the situation. Brilee was sad, but enjoyed spending some time with family, as Canyon and I began to plan Christa's funeral.

Even though I knew Christa would end up dying at a young age, I didn't plan anything ahead of time. Looking back, I wish I had, but I didn't. When we were picking out the details, I remember trying to get the cheapest casket possible. I even considered a wicker basket that they made for infants, because it was a lot cheaper. God really showed up in that moment. The funeral director kinda talked us out of the wicker basket option, so we went with a white child casket. God provided for us, because when the casket came in, they told us it was damaged. They said, if you're okay with the damage, they will give it to you for free. If not, they'll overnight a new one. We took the free option, and I could hardly even tell it was damaged. God showed up again. I was standing there, looking at a casket for my daughter, yet felt a sense of joy knowing God was taking care of us. The days in between her death and her funeral felt agonizing. I wanted closure. It bothered me to know my daughter's body was still lying there somewhere. I wanted to say my final goodbye.

Before her public funeral, I offered for my ex-husband to go to a private viewing of her. I tried to avoid drama on the day of her public viewing, so I figured if he did a private viewing, he probably wouldn't show up to the public one. I told him he could come to a private viewing if he didn't bring anyone with him. I wanted it to be the least amount of drama possible. Canyon, my mom, and I were there the day of the private viewing. My ex-husband walked up to the building, the greeter said hi and he passed by him and said "where is she?!" He appeared to be angry. Then an older woman came around the corner yelling at him to slow down. I realized I had recognized who the older woman was. I remembered her because I had witnessed in the past how she would talk so badly of people to my ex-husband's mom. When I saw her, I knew there would be drama at some point before she left. My ex-husband went into the room, saw her in the casket and dropped to the floor crying and moaning. I don't know for sure if it was guilt, but I do know it was genuine. At that point he wasn't saying anything to me. I actually felt kind of bad for him. The woman who came with him, finally caught up to him and started saying "he needs his momma I'm going outside to get her". I said "no you're not, he's fine, I asked him to come alone. He can stay here, but no one else can come in". She kept going on and on about it saying things like "that baby wasn't abused, look at him, he didn't abuse her." She was completely ignoring my ex-husband who was clearly trying to grieve, and I just lost it. I started yelling at her. I yelled "how dare you come in here and talk to me like this at my daughter's casket? This is my daughter, not yours, you don't care about her at all! Leave!" She wouldn't move, she just kept on. I started to just yell "leave" in her face over and over until she slowly started backing out. My ex-husband then started yelling and recording me on his phone. I yelled and cussed at her until she finally walked out of the room. I don't agree with how I acted now, but in that moment, I didn't care about the possible consequences. My ex-husband then turned his attention to me and started yelling about how her stone better say his last name on it. I said "fine, if that will make you happy, I'll include your last name on it". I didn't include his name in Christa's obituary because I knew if I exposed his name, he would have tons of people harassing him. They finally left, and later I found out the woman on the way out was harassing my husband Canyon saying we didn't have a miscarriage, we aborted our baby and posted photos to get attention, and crazy stuff like that. That was the drama that I was trying to avoid all together. I was just glad it happened before the public funeral, which none of his family or friends showed up to thankfully.

Christa's funeral was very peaceful, along with her burial. It was hard knowing I would never see her again. She looked so beautiful. I put a bracelet on her that said sister, and gave Brilee one to match. I put a necklace on her that said daughter, and I wore one that said mother. I put a sparrow figurine in her casket and I got one for myself to keep. The Bible verse about the sparrow always brought me comfort throughout Christa's life. The burial brought me a little comfort; I was just glad to have it all over with.

The weeks and months after she passed were particularly challenging. I cried the most when I would go into her room. I knew eventually I would have to clean it out, but I wanted to give myself plenty of time, because once it was gone, I wouldn't be able to get it back. I would go into her room and smell her bed and her pillow. It smelled just like her. That smell was a trigger for me, and would cause all of my emotions to come out. I believe letting my emotions out played a big role in my healing. Canyon held me every night, sometimes for hours, as I cried. I had imagined myself getting better sleep at night after Christa passed away, but it didn't work out how I had imagined. For years, my body was used to Christa waking me up through the night, so it was still on alert even though she was gone. I had to learn how to sleep through the night again. I also felt a lot of anger. I was so angry at my ex-husband. I felt a different type of anger once she passed away, that I had never felt before. It was an anger coming from deep in my soul it felt like. I wasn't expecting to feel so much hate towards my ex-husband. I was beyond pissed that Christa was dead because of what he did. I kept playing scenarios in my head of him allowing her to lie alone having seizures and a stroke. I imagined her thinking "mommy help me". I had to really learn how to get control of my thoughts and emotions. Holding onto all of that didn't help me, it only hurt me. I had to learn how to let it go. I had to learn to walk through the storm and face my emotions, instead of trying to find ways to bypass the storm. God helped me get through it.

Canyon ended up having to quit his job as a caregiver, to stay home with Brilee and I as we walked through grief together. We didn't have any savings, we didn't have a plan. We just knew we needed to be together. Brilee would cry every time Canyon would leave for work. I felt like I couldn't handle my own grief plus Brilee's, so he quit his job to help us. We struggled financially, but our emotional needs were met, and that season didn't last forever. The weeks turned into months, and at the time of writing this Christa has been gone for about a year and a half. Throughout this time, we have experienced a lot of healing. What I felt like would never get better, has gotten better. We have moved on in life, but there is still not a day that goes by that I don't think about Christa.

Section 2: Lessons Learned Through Shaken Baby Syndrome

I guarantee if you read the following section of this book, you will find something to help you get through a trial in your life. The lessons I'm sharing with you are lessons I learned going through many trials. If you apply the action steps I give, you will experience true transformation, whether you're going through a trial now, or you're not yet but will in the future. Your trials may be different from mine, but most of the same action steps can be applied, no matter what type of trial it is.

Lesson number 1: Trials can happen to anyone.

Have you ever experienced a situation where you felt like you were the only one going through something like it? I got married at age 19, and really the only reason we got married was because I was pregnant with our first child. I knew that my, at that time husband, was an abusive person, but I had no idea to what extent that abuse would change my life forever. I found myself thinking throughout my marriage that I was the only one who had a husband like that. That I was the only one who was pregnant and afraid. I felt that I was the only one who felt rejected, unloved, uncared for by my own spouse.

Have you ever or watched a movie or TV show where the woman was being abused and think to yourself "She's dumb. Why would she ever stay with that person? No one would ever talk to me that way. I would never allow someone around my children who acts that way." I also had those thoughts whenever I watched movies that showed domestic abuse. What I didn't realize is in most cases, it happens slowly. It doesn't start out by the person just smacking them around. It starts out slowly, and the abuse grows and grows until they are trapped in an abusive relationship. I didn't learn the lesson that trials can happen to anyone until trials happened to me. I also learned the lesson that maybe they didn't happen to me, but they happened FOR me.

Do you know someone who when you met them, your first impression was they were a great person? You thought they were someone you'd like to spend time with. You spent time with them, then you realized this person wasn't who they said they were. They weren't actually someone you want to spend your time with. That is how it happened for me, in my first marriage. That is how I ended up feeling stuck in an abusive marriage. Domestic violence is a serious issue, and a very difficult trial to go through. A lot of times people get stuck in an abusive relationship, and they don't speak out about it because the abuse gets worse when they do. It can be very difficult to speak out about what you're going through when you are going through it. I can speak about this now because I made it through it, and my abuser no longer has control over me and is no longer a thorn in my side. I am able to speak out, but there are many people who can't speak out because of the chains their abuser has put on them.

If you have found yourself, whether it's in the past or you're currently in a position where you have experienced domestic violence, I want you to know that it does happen to other people and it can happen to anyone. Domestic Abuse does not pick and choose based on income, race, religion, all of these things, it does not discriminate. It can happen to anyone. If you are feeling any shame over what you went through or what you are going through, it is time to release that shame. God can take it off of your shoulders. He can give you strength to do whatever is needed in your specific situation to be able to either forgive yourself or forgive the person, or maybe both. I hope you will spend a lot of time in prayer over this. If you have already moved on and your domestic violence situation no longer affects you in any way, this may not resonate with you. But for those who may be carrying some shame, fear, and putting up walls that affect your relationships because of what happened. I want you to be able to release this through the power of prayer. Here are three specific things to pray for every single day that are going to help you be able to be focused on this and be able to set these intentions every single day so that you can release whatever it is that still has an effect in your life.

The first thing I want you to pray is; Lord, thank You. Thank you for who you are. Thank you that no matter what choices I make, no matter what choices other people make, no matter what is happening in my life, you never leave me and you never change. I just want to say thank you. Thank you for showing up in my life. Thank you for protecting me. Thank you for forgiveness. Thank you for dying for me. Thank you for the ability to release shame through your name. Amen.

The second thing is praying for others. Lord, I pray for any woman who may be in an abusive situation or going through a trial right now. I pray that You would give her a way out, or a way through it. I pray that You would help her to see that she is strong enough and that she is loved by you. I ask that you would put opportunities on her path to help her break through strongholds. I pray that if she has children, that you help protect them and protect her. I ask that you would help her to find comfort and peace in this in whatever situation she may be in. Amen.

The third thing is moving forward. Lord, I pray that, in my situation, in this experience, I pray that you would help me to move forward. I pray that you would break down any walls that I have put up for protection. Thank you so much for helping me to protect myself and giving me a brain that is so fascinating that it's able to put up walls when needed so I can protect myself. But at this point, I am no longer in danger. So please help my brain to rewire itself to be able to let go, release any shame, any guilt, any fear around the situation, and to move forward in life. Lord, please help me to be able to share with others if needed, so that I can use my experiences for good. Amen.

I hope that you can apply this lesson and prayers to your life by inserting whatever the issue is in your life. If it's not domestic violence, maybe it's something else like your spouse going through pornography addiction, or financial issues, maybe you're going through a miscarriage, or an issue with your children. These are all things that sometimes we go through life thinking they will never happen to us. Like the lesson I had to learn, trials can happen to anyone, and the more time we spend in prayer and God's word, the better we are equipped to make it through the trial, better than we were before. Becoming aware that trials can happen to anyone, can help bring us comfort. You can't have control over everything in your life, but you can control how you react to every situation you find yourself in. Knowing you have full control over how you react to things, can help you feel comfort through the storm. You can make it through the storm with God's help, and you have the power to rise up from the ashes.

Here are a few questions to ask yourself before moving on to lesson 2:
-Do I feel that I am the only one going through the specific trial I am going through?

-If so, who is someone who is going through something similar? What book can I read?

Who can I reach out to? What YouTube channel can I binge on the topic? Can I allow it to provide me with comfort, knowing I am not alone?

-Who can I ask for support? Who can I ask to pray for me?

-Who is someone going through something similar who I can pray for?

-How can I spend more time reading God's word for encouragement?

Lesson number 2: it's okay to ask for help.

Have you ever been in a situation where you went without a need being met because you didn't want to ask for help? Maybe you've been there more times than you can count. There have been times in my life, for example, when I did that very thing. I was newly married to my first husband, and I knew I was in an abusive relationship. I knew that I had a pastor who would have been willing to talk about it. I knew I could have been in counseling. I knew there were a lot of things that could have helped me through that situation, but I refused to ask for help. Have you ever struggled with coming across as someone who is needy? That was my excuse for not asking for help, I didn't want to be "needy". It can also be difficult to reach out for help because of the fear of rejection, hearing someone say no.

The fear of judgment may also be something that could hold you back from asking for help. Maybe you've asked someone for help, and instead of offering help, they made you feel even worse because they judged you. Holding on to the belief that asking for help means you're weak is another reason you may not want to ask for help when it's needed. For example, I don't remember witnessing the women in my family asking for help, even though I knew they could have used help in different situations. I viewed them as strong women, who never needed help. Somewhere along the way, I adopted the belief, or attitude, that I could do everything on my own as a strong, independent woman. I never witnessed the value that asking for help holds. Is that the belief you hold? Do you believe that asking for help is a sign of weakness?

When going through a trial, you may find yourself in a position where you have no choice but to ask for help. You may find yourself in a position where you need financial help, emotional support, spiritual help, physical help, and that's okay. During my time of needing help, I found it more difficult to ask for emotional help than any other type of help. It can be difficult to tell people how we are truly feeling in the moment. Social media has in some cases made this harder on us. Watching others live what seems to be a perfect life, with no emotional issues going on, can cause us to question if how we are feeling is okay, or if it's just us being dramatic.

Asking for help can also bring up the emotion called shame. After Christa was injured, I got to the point where I had to ask for financial help or I would've been homeless. My daughters and I were living with my grandmother, and she was very sick. Eventually, I realized staying at her house was causing her health issues to worsen. Christa was crying so much due to her brain injury and stomach issues, and even though my grandmother never said anything, I knew it was too much for her to handle. I had to find somewhere to go, and that wasn't going to happen without asking for help. Even though I truly needed help, I still felt shame around asking for it. I ended up asking my church for help, and they showed up for me and helped my daughters and I move into an apartment.

What is it for you? What is something in your life right now that you know you should be asking for help with? This doesn't have to be a major thing; it could be something small. Maybe you need to ask for help with your kids so that you can get some rest. Something that seems minor, can actually end up helping you in major ways. Rest is essential when going through a trial. This is your reminder to make rest a priority, even if that means you have to ask for help to be able to do so. Make sure that you are open to the fact that sometimes you do need to ask for help, and that it's okay. Don't allow yourself to be held back from certain opportunities in your life just because you don't want to ask for help. It starts with being aware that you need to ask for help, then asking for help, and then receiving help when it comes. If you don't ask, people won't know how they can help you. For example, after Christa passed away, I asked our church for help. I asked them for help with my daughter Brilee through counseling. At the time. I did not have the money to spend on counseling, which I felt that she needed at the time. I had to be willing to ask for help. They were able to fulfill that need, but they wouldn't have been able to if I never asked. Sometimes, it may be a no when you ask for help. If it is, that's okay too.

If you hold a belief about asking for help being bad, receiving a no can feed the fear around asking for help. There will always be someone God will put onto your path, who will be willing to help you in whatever way He sees fit. You may have to push past a lot of fear to allow this person into your life. Are you willing to receive help? Receiving help could look like going to counseling, going to a support group, reading a book someone gives you and applying the knowledge, accepting money from someone offering it to you, allowing someone to watch your kids while you take care of your own needs, and so on.

There is always someone out there willing to help in a way but it may require you some work on your end. Someone may help meet your needs. Someone may answer your call for help, but you may also have to be open to doing some type of work. This can look like someone offering to help you financially, and along with giving you money they ask for you to take a free financial class their church offers. Your need for money is met, but you also have to put forth the effort of taking the financial class the person suggested. It may also look like someone offering to babysit for you now, and one day in the future you repay them by babysitting their child when they need it. This could also look like going to counseling for emotional help, and the counselor giving you homework. You're receiving the emotional help you asked for, and also working to better yourself through completing the homework.

In case no one has ever told you this, you deserve help. You were created to have relationships with other people, to create community, to have people around you to help you to love you. You are loved and you are deserving of help that God puts in your path. Release any belief that you may have that you're not worthy of help and that help is not good. Allow help to come into your life because your new belief is it is okay to ask for help. It is okay to be on rock bottom and to ask for a hand up. Be aware that there are times that God may allow people to say no to you. He may not put someone on your path to help you because he may be trying to grow you. There have been times where I have asked for help, and it just seemed like no matter what, I was not getting the help that I was asking for. Let's just say for example, financially. Let's say that I needed $2,000 And it just seemed like no matter who I asked it just wasn't coming to me. If something like that happens to you, you may need to take a step back and ask yourself, "do I really truly need this help? Or is there a way I can make this happen on my own?" You may find that it may be something that God is trying to show you through your experience, through allowing you to go without in that particular area. You can ask yourself, "What could God be teaching me?" You can pray and ask God to reveal that to you as well.

Back to my example of needing $2,000. If I kept receiving "no" from people, I may have asked myself "this is clearly a no, so how can I make it happen? How can I make this $2,000 that I need?" There has to be an opportunity out there. Then I shift my prayers from God, please send me someone to help me to God How can I make this happen? What can I do? Is there anything that you want me to do? Anything you want me to learn? What can I do for this $2,000 to come into my life? The best way to get better at asking for help is to start asking for help. Like building muscle, it gets easier over time. Break through the limiting beliefs by taking a step to ask for something minor, and lead up to asking for something major. We all need help at some point. There's not one person on this earth that at some point has not needed some type of help and had to ask for it. They also had to be open to receiving it.

Here are some different things that I did to help my negative mindset around asking for help, that I believe can help you as well. Number one, learn about how the brain works. Learning how the mind works and how you can pick up beliefs throughout your life, and carry them into adulthood. Have you ever realized some of the things you believe, you believe just because it's what you were told when you were younger, or something you saw on tv? Once you become aware of the fact that those limiting beliefs could have come from anywhere, you can begin to question them.

If you are feeling resistance towards asking for help, ask yourself "why do I feel this resistance? Where did this come from? Did this come from my childhood? Did this come from a time where I asked for help and someone told me no?"

After questioning it, trying to pinpoint where you got that specific belief, examine if it is real or if it's something that you can let go of and change. If you realize you did get a belief from childhood, ask yourself "does this belief serve me"?

For example, my belief of asking for help being a sign of weakness did not serve me in any way whenever I was sitting in the ICU with my daughter, and I needed a break. I needed to be able to walk out of the ICU room, because I hadn't been out of there in days. I had to make a decision, to allow my belief to hold me back, release that belief that I had from childhood and allow someone to sit with Christa so I could take a break.

When you become aware that this is an issue for you, you can begin praying about it specifically. Ask God to reveal to you what He would like for you to do. Ask Him if you should ask for help, or if He wants you to do it on your own. Ask if He will provide for your needs in whatever way He sees fit. Ask Him for the strength you need to either ask for help or do it on your own, with His help. Ask God to reveal to you if a limiting belief is holding you back. Asking God to reveal things to you sometimes means you have to be still. You may have to sit with it, sit with yourself, and sit with God long enough to be able to discern what he might be trying to tell you.

Once you do receive the help that you're asking for, be intentional about showing gratitude for it. When you show gratitude for the help you've received, more is going to come into your life. You can pray and let God know how much you appreciate all He has given you. Maybe He helped you leave an abusive marriage, maybe He helped you get out of debt, maybe He provided childcare when you needed it, maybe He softened your heart for you to be able to work towards saving your marriage, maybe He provided a car when you needed one, and so on. Go on a rampage of gratitude for all He has provided for you. You will find that even when you're in a trial, you still have many things to be grateful for. Being grateful can improve your mood, along with attracting more help and opportunities into your life. Everyone likes to hear thank you, and I believe God likes to hear it too. Grab a sticky note and write down Psalm 9:1 "I will give thanks to You, Lord, with all my heart; I will tell of all Your wonderful deeds". This will help remind you to constantly thank the Lord for what He has done in your life.

When asking people for help, it's likely they will be more willing to help you more than once when you go above and beyond to show gratitude.

Here are a few ways you can do that:
-send a thank you card

-pray for them/with them

-send them a letter acknowledging everything they've done for you

-invite them to have dinner with you

-offer to do something for them

-send them something encouraging

-keep a journal of people who have helped you in case you'd like to repay them in the future

It's amazing how far a thank you card can go when showing gratitude. Showing gratitude is important, even if you know they will never be able to help you again, because it can help the person who is helping you, by giving them the gift of fulfillment.

Here are a few questions to ask yourself before moving on to lesson 3:

-Do I struggle with asking for help?

-Am I holding onto any limiting beliefs around asking for help?

-If so, where did those limiting beliefs come from?

-Do these beliefs serve me or hold me back? Can I let go of the negative ones?

-Am I asking God for His help in my situation?

What is one thing I can ask for help with right now?

-How will I benefit from asking for help with it?

-How will those around me benefit from me asking for help?

-Am I showing gratitude for what I currently have?

-Where can I add a "gratitude rampage" into my schedule?

-What are some things I can do to go above and beyond to show gratitude for those who help me?

-How will I follow through with those things?

Lesson Number 3: God's timing is perfect.

God's timing is perfect and it may not be my timing. That phrase may be difficult for you to accept when you're going through a trial. I'm going to be very open and vulnerable about how this phrase affected me. Many times, I wondered when God would relieve my daughter Christa of her pain. I wondered when he would take her back to heaven with Him, so she would suffer no more. At the time, I didn't want to admit that, and felt bad asking for God to take her. I was experiencing anguish because of the daily pain that she was going through. I questioned God's timing and eventually I had to realize that God's timing was perfect. I had to submit to that and leave it to him to decide when the timing was right for Christa's life on earth to be over.

I discovered I wasted a lot of time questioning God about His timing. I asked Him questions such as: "why aren't you doing anything? Why is this happening? Why won't you help her? When are you going to end this suffering?" I now wish I would've been asking more "how" questions. "How will you work this for our good? How can I help her? How can I help end her suffering here on earth while we wait for you to end her suffering forever in heaven?" Christa had her feeding tube replaced under anesthesia once every 3 months. When the procedure was being done, I would ask God "Can you please take her whenever she's under anesthesia?" To me, that would've been the easiest way for her to pass away. That was me questioning God's timing, and God's plan. I didn't truly want her to pass away and I didn't want it to be like that. Maybe God allowed that request to go unanswered because He was actually protecting me. I look back now, and see He could've been protecting me from carrying guilt for the rest of my life over her death. If she had died under anesthesia, I would've questioned if I made the right decision to allow her to have the procedure done. I would've questioned if it was truly God's timing and plan. She never had issues with anesthesia and that was not how she passed away. The way she did pass away left me with no doubt at all that it was God's timing and plan.

I tell you all of this to make a point. The point is, in the thick of the trial I was going through, desperation kicked in. If I had things my way during those moments, it would've ruined God's greater plan. Emotions can be so strong that they are louder than truth. God's word makes it clear that His ways are not our ways, and that He's always working on our behalf even when we can't see or hear His voice. Know that if you're in the thick of the trial you're going through, your emotions are valid. It can be difficult to remind yourself of biblical truth, but it is possible. You can stand on God's word. It's okay to question what God is doing in your life, but never doubt that He is good. You may have to constantly remind yourself of God's timing being perfect, because there is a lot of noise when going through a trial. The devil and the world want to drown out the voice of God, the voice of truth, especially when you're most vulnerable. Fight back by keeping your focus on God and His word.

There are also times in life where God calls us into a season of waiting. Waiting on the Lord is not easy, but a lot of value can be found in a period of waiting. I will give you a personal example of a season of waiting. Not long after Christa was injured, I began a season of waiting on the Lord for a husband. I was not yet divorced from Christa's biological father, so my intentions were to build friendships, and once I was divorced, get into a romantic relationship. My divorce was "supposed" to be fast, according to my attorney, and be finalized a few months after it was filed. I felt very hopeful and excited to break free from the marriage and man I was married to. As I waited, I started a friendship with my now husband, Canyon. After getting to know him, I felt God was telling me that Canyon was going to be my husband. In my mind, I thought I would be divorced within three months from filing, and not long after that God would send me Canyon. I found out the hard way that was not what God had planned for me. Three months turned into a year. During the year I waited for my divorce to be final, I grew weary and felt hopeless many times. I began to question if I'd ever be granted a divorce, and if I'd ever be able to start a relationship with Canyon. God kept reassuring me, but I grew sick of waiting. I was a single mom, providing for my children, and a caregiver for Christa. I felt so overwhelmed and I begged God for someone to help me. I always wanted to be a wife, and I couldn't understand in the moment why God was making me wait. I took things into my own hands, and rushed into a relationship with someone who I met online. After a few months, I realized I had made a mistake. I broke off the relationship, and my heart was hurting. I knew God would give Canyon to me to be my husband, but during that waiting season, there were no physical signs. Canyon had made it clear that he was not interested in a romantic relationship with me, and that we were just friends. After the heartache I had caused myself, I ran back to God and spent time in prayer surrendering my love life, and everything else, to Him. I remember sitting on the floor of my small apartment crying telling God I was sorry, and I would do anything He wanted me to do. I accepted my season of singleness. I can look back now and see so many lessons I learned while being a single mom, that I wouldn't have learned if Canyon had been my husband at the time. Those times of strength and complete reliance on God still inspire and motivate me to this day. About 4 months after completely surrendering the "Canyon situation" to God, Canyon came into my life permanently. What started as a conversation between friends right after my grandmother passed away, turned into a serious relationship and then marriage. God had delivered, but only in His timing, not mine.

Maybe you are in a season of waiting. I want to encourage you to spend time in prayer asking God to reveal to you what he wants you to do, or what he doesn't want you to do. Ask Him what He wants you to stop doing or what He wants you to start doing. When He does reveal something to you, go through with it. If He doesn't reveal anything, then you should also be quiet and still, and wait on the Lord. It says in the Bible to wait on the Lord. If you are feeling down about being in a season of waiting, take a sticky note and write out different verses about your situation to help remind you that waiting also happened in the Bible. Leave those reminders on your mirror, on your wall, on your fridge, or wherever you look every day to refresh your memory on the fact that God's got your situation under control.

Another thing you could do is find others who are in a season of waiting.

It can be nice to have a friend who might be in the same situation that you're in. As long as it's not a toxic friendship, where you both keep yourselves down, and one gets jealous of the other when one gets ahead, it can be healing. That type of friendship can help you feel seen and heard. A solid friendship helps you feel validated as well, because waiting on the Lord can be hard. I want to validate that for you right now. It is very hard to wait. Finding the right friend can help you feel comfort, and it also helps you have accountability. Find a prayer buddy where you both come up with one day a week and you call each other and you pray for each other in your situations. That will develop a bond that lasts forever because hopefully one day you will both look back and think "wow". You cared for each other when you both were at one of your lowest times, and look what God has done since then. God's timing is perfect, even if it means we have to go through a season of waiting. His timing is not always our timing, and His ways are not always our ways.

Here are a few questions to ask yourself before moving on to lesson 4:

-Can I ask more "how" questions while going through this trial?

-Am I allowing my emotions to be louder than Truth?

-How can I remind myself daily of God's truth?

-How can I find others going through a similar situation?

-What can I do to cultivate friendships?

-Am I praying, asking God to bring good friends into my life?

-When can I schedule time to pray with and for my friends?

Lesson number 4: rejection does not equal your worth.

Can you remember a time in your life where you felt rejected by someone close to you? Maybe it was your parents, maybe a sibling, a friend at school, a coach, or someone at church. When you experienced the rejection, it made you question your worth. I have experienced this many times in my life, and for me, it seems rejection stings more when I'm more vulnerable, going through a trial. I personally struggled with my self-worth and the rejection of my now ex-husband. So much time was wasted, and opportunities not taken because I believed what he said about me. I allowed his words and the rejection to become part of my identity.

When rejection comes from someone close to you, it can cut even deeper.
For example, during our marriage, my ex-husband would reject me whenever I asked him for money. He would withhold money from me and use it to control me. At the time, he worked full time and I worked part time as a licensed massage therapist, so he made more than I did. When the time would come to pay bills or buy something I needed, since he wouldn't share a bank account with me, I would ask him for the money to do so. He would either say no, or would only give it to me under certain conditions that he laid out for me to follow. I allowed that rejection to lower my self-worth and make me question why I wasn't "good enough" to

receive money from him. I also felt like I wasn't good enough to make more money on my own, or even have relationships with people who made more money, since I didn't make much. I allowed the rejection to deeply penetrate my thoughts and eventually my identity. There was a constant spiritual battle going on as well. I knew who God said I was, but I allowed the world to cloud His view of me. Stop for a moment to think if you are in that place. Has the world's opinion of you drowned out who God says you are? Maybe you're thinking to yourself "why am I never good enough for you?" "What is wrong with me?" There will be times you will never know why someone is rejecting you. It could be as simple as they just had an argument with their spouse, they didn't sleep well the past few nights, or you remind them of someone they didn't like in the past. The reason why could be a number of things. Here is permission to stop blaming yourself.

Another thing to be aware of is rejection doesn't automatically mean the person doing the rejecting doesn't care about or love you. Sometimes it does, but often that person doesn't even realize what they're doing, or not doing. It is important for you to set your own boundaries to protect your heart. If someone who, you know loves you, keeps making you feel rejected by them, find a healthy way to protect yourself from them. You don't have to completely cut them out of your life. You may decide to limit time spent around them or be intentional about spending extra time praying before and after you're around them. The stronger your self-worth, the easier it will be to be around people like this.

The best way to strengthen your self-worth is by finding it through Jesus. He gives us plenty of verses and stories in the Bible to confirm that we are worthy of Him and His love. Jesus died for you. Think about how much worth you must have if He thought you were worth dying for. Don't allow your self-worth to be lowered by this world and people's opinions. Finding your self-worth in God alone can help you break any chains that others' opinions may have on you. You can begin the process of finding your worth in God alone by praying, asking for His help.

Pray this over yourself: Lord, thank you so much for creating me. Thank you so much for my life. Thank you for these years that I have had. I am sorry for the times that I allowed the world and man to cause me to think less of myself. I want you to help me see myself the way you see me, Lord, I want to see myself as who your word says I am.
Please help me release any fear of rejection. Help me release rejection when it does come my way. We know that it's going to come, please help me to be able to cope with it well. Help me to be able to stand strong on your word. When I do feel doubt about myself and begin to question my self-worth, I pray that you will help me fight it. I ask that you'll give me strength, that you will remind me and comfort me. Remind me of who you say I am.

Thank you, Lord, amen.

There are also so many encouraging resources, other than the Bible, although the Bible is the number one resource for me when it comes to facing rejection and self-worth. I want to encourage you, if you find yourself giving in to rejection and allowing it to affect who you are and your worth, find a book, podcast, YouTube channel, etc, where someone, who is a Christian who believes in Biblical truth, is speaking out about self-worth, and self-doubt. Allow what they have to say to start changing the way you view yourself. Let it uplift you. Put their advice into practice.

During a time where I faced a lot of rejection and self-doubt issues, I listened to a podcast called The Mommy Millionaire Show hosted by Cayla Craft. Her confidence, self-worth, discipline, motivation, and Godliness inspired me through some of my darkest days. She helped me believe in myself and know if she could work through her past and difficult times, then I could too. I recommend her podcast if you're looking for something to help uplift you.

If you are currently struggling with your self-worth, look at yourself in the mirror and repeat this sentence: I allow rejection to increase my self-awareness. I am good at coping with rejection. I find my self-worth in Christ. I love myself. I allow rejection to help me grow. Affirmations, without some type of action behind them, are just words. But if you put an action behind it, such as prayer, that would be an action to those affirmations.

Another example could be exercising. If you doubt yourself because of your weight, and you want to change that, you can't just say the words and lose the weight. You have to take action by working out and eating healthy. That is how affirmations are meant to work. Other actions may include seeing a counselor, meditating on God's word, or taking time for self-care. Speaking life over yourself and putting action behind your words can help you begin to release rejection and find your self-worth in Christ.

Here are a few questions to ask yourself before moving on to lesson 5:

-Can I think of a time I was rejected by someone close to me?

-If so, how did I allow that to affect me?

-Have I allowed the rejection to doubt my self-worth?

-What beliefs do I carry about myself, and did they come from the rejection?

-If so, how can I release the rejection and their opinion about me?

-What new beliefs will I have about myself?

-What does God say about my self-worth?

-How can I give myself grace, and remind myself of these new beliefs daily?

-What actions can I take daily to increase my self-worth?

Lesson number 5: community matters.

Before my experience with Shaken Baby Syndrome and going through trials, I did not realize how important community was and having people around me who cared for me and my kids. Because I was in such an abusive marriage and controlling marriage, I was not able to create relationships around me. I did not have many friends and I was not a reliable person. So, when my daughter was shaken, I had four or five friends who I could rely on, and it wasn't until then that I experienced the importance of having a church family as well.

If you're going through a trial right now, you are probably realizing how important it is to create relationships, and you're probably feeling a lot of gratitude for the ones that you already do have in your life. I want to encourage you to be open to different types of relationships and new friendships during this time especially.

God will send you people who will care for you who will love you, so be open to that.

If needed, ask God to help you with that. There is a verse in the Bible that talks about you have not because you ask not. When was the last time that you asked God for a new relationship for a new friendship?

I realized the importance of this going through shaken baby syndrome, because I was in a position where it hurt so badly, I could hardly even pray for myself. I could hardly find the strength to pray for my daughter. It was one of those times where it felt like all I could say was Jesus. Jesus tells us in the Bible that if we call out his name, he will go to the throne on our behalf. It's also nice to have a church group who you can call upon to pray for you. There may come a time where you are just feeling so down. You're on rock bottom. You feel so desperate and you don't know what to do. It hurts so badly that you may not even be able to pray. That's when your community comes in and wraps their arms around you, comforts you, and shows up for you.

I grew up in a church named First Church of the Nazarene in Lenoir City. I grew very close to the pastor there. His name is Pastor David Smith. He was with me and my family through all of my worst trials of life. He showed up for everything. The entire community at that church always showed up for me no matter what. My dad passed away when I was 13, and Pastor David was at the hospital when we told my dad goodbye. The same for when we told my grandmother goodbye when she passed away, and also through the most difficult times with Christa. He came in the middle of the night when we called saying Christa was going to pass away soon. That is the importance of having a church family. That church prayed for me more times than I can count, and I didn't even go to that church very often in my adult life. But they never stopped rallying around me in my time of need and my daughter's time of need. That was priceless. Without my community, I would've felt so alone.

Going through a trial is also a great time to develop new relationships.
When my daughter was first injured and in the PICU, I had visitors from a church called First Baptist Concord. I didn't know those people at all, but because I was open to it, God sent them to me. Meeting new people while you're experiencing something painful may sound horrible. I can promise you that if you will just let it happen, you will look back and be thankful you did. If I had said "no" when the nurse asked me if I wanted a visitor, my life would've been and still would be a lot different. I didn't ask them to come to the hospital, they just came. They could have made 100 excuses of why they shouldn't. They could have been like "oh, she's probably too tired". Another excuse could've been "we shouldn't go there, we don't even know her, what if we scare her off?" They could have made the excuses but they listened to God telling them to show up for me and to show up at that hospital and to speak to me. Because they listened and they were obedient to God, and because I was obedient to God as far as allowing them in, a beautiful community was created. I tell you these details because I want to show you how truly important it is to have good people around you. You can only have good people around you when you are open and receptive to it, which takes intention.

Here is another example of how God will send you someone when you need them.

There were a few times that my daughter had major surgery on her bowels.

One of those times I was at the hospital alone with her. I was sitting in the waiting room by myself and I was having a little bit of a pity party. I was thinking "I hate this, it is not fair". I asked, "God, why would you allow this to happen to me? Why would you allow me to be sitting here alone at one of the worst times of my life? This is horrible. I don't want to be here alone." I just kept going on and on about how I wish I had a husband or someone to be here for these things. I then saw this older gentleman walking towards me who was a volunteer at the hospital. I was thinking "please don't talk to me". He sat down next to me and started talking. As I listened, he reminded me of this sweet grandfather that I would love to have had in my life. Something about him was so comforting. He just talked about normal things, and allowed me to talk about whatever I wanted to talk about. His name was Jay Alexander. He made such a difference in my life because after that conversation, anytime I would see Jay in the hospital, he would remember me and he would ask about my daughter and my family. I would look for him any time we were at the hospital. He brought comfort to what can be such a lonely place. There were also several nurses at that hospital who did the same. One nurse specifically, Carrie Davis, who would work the night shift. Every time Christa was admitted to the PICU, I hoped Carrie would be her nurse. What I want you to take from this is that none of these examples I gave would've been reality had I not allowed people in. It's most difficult to allow people in when you're hurting.

I want to encourage you, though it can be hard, be friendly even when you're going through a trial. Your relationships matter. It's not all about just taking from these relationships, you're also going to give to them. But you may be in a trial right now where you have to take a lot and you're having to ask for a lot. For example, I had a friend that I met through church, and the place that I worked at. Her name was Season Henry. She was an amazing person who came into my life and helped me a lot with my daughter Brilee. Not only was I a single mom who had to work, but I was also caring for Brilee. When Christa was placed on hospice care, I knew it wouldn't be long before she passed away. Doctors couldn't give us a time frame, but I had a feeling it wouldn't be long. One day I went out for a drive to have some alone time. As I was driving, I suddenly had the thought (which I believe was from God) to pull over and text Season, asking for help with Brilee. I texted her "hey, I don't know if you have plans for fall break, but Christa has been put on hospice care and I am feeling overwhelmed. Can you help me with brilee?" When she replied that she was in another state on vacation, I felt down and like my "gut feeling" to text her was wrong. Later that day, she called me asking if Brilee wanted to vacation with them for the week. One of her friends was heading that way the next day, and offered to take Brilee, so she went.

HOW AMAZING IS GOD?

Little did I know, Christa would pass away that week. I didn't know, but God knew. My sweet Brilee was able to go to the beach and have a great time relieving me of worrying about her being home while Christa passed away. I am so thankful she didn't have to witness that. Here's what I want you to know from that story; 1. Sometimes that thought you randomly have is from God. Be sure to follow through with what He tells you to do. 2. When you're going through a trial, let God know the desires of your heart. I let Him know that I didn't want Brilee around, and He delivered in the most beautiful, unexpected way. 3. Trust God's plan, no matter what happens. His timing may not be your timing and His ways not your ways.

Another cool thing God did for us during that time was providing shelter for our puppy. A few weeks before Christa was placed on hospice care, we took our puppy to a trainer. Once I found out Christa was being placed on hospice care, I reached out to the trainer asking her if she could help us in any way. She let me know the kennel she worked at was willing to keep our puppy as long as we needed them to, FOR FREE. That was a huge relief because we didn't have the money to pay for someone to keep her, and she would've gotten in our way a lot especially during Christa's final hours.

All of these blessings started with creating a relationship. This is why community is so important. You get the blessing of serving your community when they need you, but also there may come a time where you need them. I want to give you a few ways that you can start creating relationships. The biggest way that I have been able to create relationships with people is getting involved in a church. Most churches are going to understand that you're there to create relationships, and it makes it a lot easier. The whole point of going to a small group is to get to know each other. That was a lot less intimidating for me than it was going to a park with my daughter and just trying to create friendships there. You can also do things like joining social media groups specific to what you're going through. For example, I searched out Shaken Baby Syndrome groups because that was something very specific that I felt very alone in and it felt like no one else understood that. I also searched out miscarriage groups because that's not just a group that you really find at a church or anywhere that you go meet in person. Another way that you can help create community is going above and beyond for people and being intentional about it. Spend time in prayer for others and in prayer asking God to help you build that community. This is lesson number five that I learned through Shaken Baby Syndrome. Community matters, friendships matter, and it really isn't as hard as I thought to create these things. It's really not as scary as I once thought it was to make friends and put myself out there and to be vulnerable. It's so worth having people around you that love and care for you.

Here are a few questions to ask yourself before moving on to lesson 6:

-Am I being intentional about creating a community around me?

-If not, what can I add to my schedule to start doing this?

-Am I being a good friend to others?

-Who can I pray for daily?

-Who can I ask to pray for me?

-Is there a small group at church that I can join?

Lesson number 6: the importance of personal development.

I never realized how much I needed to change until I was faced with something that was forcing me to change. A few months after Christa was shaken, I discovered that the person God was calling me to become was found in my daily habits. Going through a trial can create a situation where change and transformation is necessary. This doesn't always happen immediately. It can take a lot of patience and grace to adapt and make the changes. Like me, you may find yourself in a position where it's not as much of a choice anymore. It could be a situation where it's you make a change, or suffer extreme consequences. One of my favorite quotes is "nothing changes if nothing changes". There have been times in my life where I have to remind myself of that constantly. I find it has been sticky note on the mirror worthy.

An easy way to get started in personal development is listening to podcasts and books about it. I do want to encourage you to be careful with what advice you follow. Don't allow personal development content to take God's place, or to lead you astray. God wants us to learn and grow, but He also wants us to fully rely and depend on Him as well. We can do both.

Prayer and reading the Bible also plays an important role in personal development. Maybe you feel like you don't know how to pray, you don't have to know how, you just have to start. Add these two things into your life daily. It takes discipline to create new habits, including spending time with God. You won't always feel like opening your Bible to study God's word. You won't always feel like making the time to get on your knees to pray. If you have self-discipline in this area and make this a priority, you will see change and transformation in your life. Determine what areas of your life you need a change in. If it's in your parenting, let go of any pride you may have, and do the work to develop that area and to get better. If it's in your finances, there are plenty of books to provide you with more than enough information on how to create habits to better your finances. Sometimes, your situation may not change, but you can change and make the situation easier on yourself.

I will give you an example of a personal situation that I have been in, where I really had to do the hard work to change, and it was not easy. The day before Christa was placed on hospice care, she vomited, which indicated to my husband and I that something was wrong. She never vomited because her feeding tube bypassed her stomach and went directly into her intestines. My husband took her to the ER while I stayed home with our other daughter Brilee. Christa was admitted overnight so they could keep an eye on her. My husband Canyon stayed with her. The next morning, a social worker asked me to go to the hospital so they could set up hospice care. The doctors had determined they believed her body was failing, the vomit was fluid from her lungs, and that she qualified for hospice care. I was actually happy about that because it finally meant she'd get the pain medication I had been fighting to get her for the past few months prior to that. Christa was discharged that evening. Canyon and I were talking like normal, when I asked to see his phone to get on Pinterest to find some ideas to decorate Christa's room for her end-of-life care. I wanted it to be a relaxing environment. It didn't take long for the algorithm on his internet to reveal to me that he had been searching and watching pornography. At first, my brain could hardly register what was happening. I was blindsided by what I was seeing. This was a big deal to me, because Canyon and I had spent a lot of time in our marriage working on healing him from his pornography addiction. He confessed to me that he had looked at it the night before. I looked at my situation as one of the worst moments of my life. My daughter had just been placed on hospice care, and I felt deeply betrayed by the one person who was supposed to care for me the most. I had to push that aside, and focus on Christa. It was only about two weeks later that Christa passed away. After that, I truly learned the importance of personal development. My marriage and life depended on it. I felt absolutely miserable. There were times I felt I would rather die than to feel such heartache. I didn't want to leave my house because I feared releasing my grief in public. I also feared seeing an attractive woman. I was so angry at women during that time. I didn't even want to see one and I definitely didn't want my husband to see one. After being in survival mode for a few months, I realized even if my husband and situation never changed, it was up to me to be happy. I had to change the way I thought. I was allowing my negative thoughts to consume me. My husband was completely open and willing and began to implement his own changes, but that wasn't enough. I also had to change. Committing to personal development saved my life and my marriage.

You may or may not be going through a trial right now, and even if you're not, there is still an area of your life that can benefit from personal development. Keeping a prayer journal gives you the ability to look back and see everything that God has done and to remind you of all the prayers he answered. This can give you motivation to keep making changes as needed. Writing things down can also help you release stress and anxiety over a situation. A book I highly recommend reading about prayer is The Circle Maker by Mark Batterson. It helped change the way I think about prayer. God is capable of working a miracle in your life. Sometimes that miracle may begin with you taking small steps towards developing yourself, to be able to receive the miracle.

Here are a few questions to ask yourself before moving on to lesson 7:

-Am I open to becoming aware of what needs to change in my life?

-How can I spend time being still, waiting for God to reveal to me what He wants me to do for personal development?

-Will I commit to making a change? What would that look like for me?

-Who is a trustworthy person that will be willing to pray with and for me as I am making this change?

-What book will I start reading for personal development?

-How will I start implementing actions for change in my daily life?

-What will making changes do for me? What happens if I don't change?

Lesson Number 7: Forgiveness

This is a major lesson I learned through Shaken Baby Syndrome. It was and is one of the hardest and most difficult lessons that I went through and learned. I learned it through God calling me and helping me to forgive my ex-husband, who was blamed for shaking our daughter. You may find yourself in a position where there's someone who God might be calling you to forgive, and you're having a very difficult time forgiving this person. Forgiving someone who has hurt you is not easy, especially if they hurt you continually.

After Christa suffered Shaken Baby Syndrome, I found myself very angry at her biological father. I was trying to do everything I could possibly do to get him put in jail and to get what I called justice. None of my efforts were working, and I was worn out. I was harboring unforgiveness, and the only person that was hurting me was me. I called the DHS office, the DA's office, and random attorneys to ask if they would help me pro-bono, because I had no money to pay for their services. I was told "no" time and time again. I felt very defeated. At the time, Christa had no nursing care, so I was her caregiver 24/7. She almost never slept and was always uncomfortable. I was exhausted trying to carry it all. I finally realized there must've been a reason I was getting so much resistance, so I had to go to God with it. The world was telling me Christa's biological father needed to go to jail, and yet no one stepped up to help accomplish that. I knew I couldn't keep going on the way I was, using any extra time I had calling attorneys. Just like I mentioned in the last lesson, I knew change was necessary, or I wouldn't survive without losing my mind. I began praying about it, and God kept putting the word forgive in front of me. I kept seeing random YouTube videos and Bible verses talking about forgiveness. I kept wrestling with it and with God. I thought "there is No way I can forgive him for this, she and I both still suffer daily". I had to be in constant prayer asking God to help change my heart. He revealed to me that forgiveness is more for me than for my ex-husband. Holding onto that anger and resentment was only hurting me, not him. He didn't have a clue how I felt and he didn't care. I had to make a decision to be obedient to what God was calling me to do.

Forgiveness does not happen overnight. It requires daily action and constant prayer in the process. You have to pray for yourself, for your heart to change. It may not seem fair to ask God to change your heart when you didn't do anything. Since we can't change others, we have to take full ownership of our feelings and emotions and sometimes that requires us to make changes. When you're going through the process of forgiving someone, you may have to adopt a mindset of forgiveness. Take every thought captive and make it obedient to the Lord.

You may have to push past your circumstances or old beliefs about forgiveness. The world may say "you have a right to be angry, to have hate in your heart towards that person, to harbor unforgiveness". You get to decide if you will listen to the world or to God's word. I can't even count the number of times I have been told "I would've killed him", when I told someone, my ex-husband shook Christa. It was never helpful, and it would annoy me honestly. I always had to remind myself that was a worldly response, not a Godly one.

I have been shamed for sharing about how I forgave my ex-husband as well. When you decide you're going to forgive someone who has hurt you, it's possible you may get backlash for it. Just remember, you don't live for them, you live for God, who you know has called you to forgive. Forgiving my ex-husband lifted a huge weight from my shoulders. It gave me more time freedom and more space in my mind. I surrendered it all to God, and trusted that He would take care of any justice as He saw fit. I have had to forgive him 7x70 times like God tells us to in the Bible. I had to deal with harassing texts from my ex-husband and doing supervised visitations with him for a few years.

Here's what I want you to know. You can forgive and also refuse to put up with wrongdoing. I forgave my ex-husband, but I did not put up with him degrading me. I blocked his phone number often. You don't have to be a doormat just because you have forgiven someone. Don't allow them to run over you. If you're in an abusive situation, you can forgive that person, but don't forgive and forget. You are in charge of keeping yourself and your children safe. Just because you forgive, does not mean you have to go back. I know the consequences of forgiving and forgetting terrible and abusive behavior. My ex-husband at times in our marriage would do drugs. Doing cocaine and meth can cause a person to do some horrible things. Each time he would do something to hurt me mentally and/or physically, he would ask for forgiveness and beg me not to leave him. I forgave him and forgot about his actions. In that situation, forgiveness did not serve me, it harmed me. I learned to forgive at a distance, and to set boundaries.

I truly believe God rewarded me for being obedient to Him. He saw my tears, He saw how much I had to go through with Christa, He was right beside me through it all. After a few years, all rights to Brilee and Christa were removed from my ex-husband. God provided my current husband, Canyon, and I with the opportunity to go to court and terminate my ex's rights, through a step-parent adoption. It was a miracle. My ex-husband tried to fight it, but ultimately God had the last say and rights were terminated. I can't help but to wonder if God would've given us that major blessing if I had harbored unforgiveness all those years. He was working on my behalf, and I had no idea. He made what seemed impossible, possible.

Forgiveness will set you free.

Questions to ask yourself after this final lesson:

-Is unforgiveness holding me back right now?

-Who do I need to forgive? How can I start the process?

–Do I need to forgive myself for something?

-After I forgive, what boundaries do I need to set and stick to?

$100 AMAZON GIFT CARD CHRISTMAS GIVEAWAY

Follow the QR code link below to enter.

You just finished this book and it may have brought a few things/feelings to your attention that you weren't aware of before. Maybe you're wondering "where should I start with working through these things?" My suggestion is starting with prayer. Right now, what can you thank God for? Who can you pray for? What can you ask God to do in your life? As you're working through things remember: trials happen to everyone, it's okay to ask for help, God's timing is perfect, rejection does not equal your worth, building community matters, personal development is important, and you have the ability to forgive. You have the power, through Christ, to make true transformation happen in your life.

Find Me Online:

(I love connecting with readers)

Instagram @sierra.m.cooke & @shaken.baby.mom

YouTube Sierra Cooke

TikTok @sierracooke

Podcast Going Through Trials with God on Spotify & Anchor

Email sierra.marie.cooke@gmail.com

Online Business / Health & Wellness Products

Please leave a review of this book on Amazon/Kindle.

Printed in Great Britain
by Amazon